THE CLASSIC DOLCI OF THE ITALIAN JEWS

THE CLASSIC DOLCI OF THE ITALIAN JEWS

A World of Jewish Desserts

by

EDDA SERVI MACHLIN

Illustrations by Lou Myers

Croton-on-Hudson GIRO PRESS Publisher

Published by:
GIRO PRESS
P.O. Box 203
Croton-on-Hudson, N.Y. 10520

ISBN 1-878857-12-6

Printed in the United States of America
First Edition

To Gene

*

For
Rona and Gia
who have always and enthusiastically
endorsed all my endeavours

*

Having enjoyed my desserts all their lives
they are the living proof that one
can indulge in them
while preserving a lovely
figure

*

ACKNOWLEDGEMENTS

I am indebted to a number of people for their dessert heirlooms, for their suggestions on the choice of recipes, for their criticisms and their encouragement. To all of those good friends and relatives go my sincere thanks. I always give credit to the contributors of recipes in the prologue to the recipes themselves. However, I want to thank in particular my brother Gino and his wife Metella, my sister Marcella and her family, and my brother Mario and his family for their warmhearted, invaluable help.

The baker Carmelinda Mazzoli, although not Jewish, inherited from the woman who took care of the Jewish community's baking needs in Pitigliano the recipes for some of our holiday sweets. She gave me two of the oldest recipes in this collection and did not hesitate to demonstrate to me how to make them. Her generosity was in character with that of her grandmother, the public baker Agatina, who defied the Fascist Racial Law and surreptitiously supplied my Mother with bread.

My warm thanks go also to Robert Rahtz, who carefully copy edited the text. However, all errors that remain are my responsibility.

Our dear friend Lou Myers deserves a special thanks for the contribution of his brilliant art work to the body of the book. Lou and his wife Bernice are unique in the pantheon of exceptionally good human beings.

FOREWORD

Before I even met Edda Servi Machlin, I had read and cooked from her delightful and impressive two volumes of *The Classic Cuisine of Italian Jews*. Here Edda gathered recipes, culture and, indeed, history that may well have been lost forever without her careful recollection. Despite the horror that Edda witnessed during the Holocaust in her native land, she has risen above this to embrace the Italian life that had been her family's for generations.

Having met her only briefly before writing my own book, *The Jewish Holiday Baker*, I knew she had to be one of the 13 cooks from around the world portrayed in the book. Thankfully, I got to know her even better during the many days I spent with her cooking and talking while we were filming for the public television series, "Jewish Cooking in America with Joan Nathan."

In this third volume of Edda's, "the icing on the cake," she has reached out beyond her native Pitigliano to encompass Italian Jewish sweets from throughout the country (and from elsewhere). These are recipes she clearly has used throughout her life. What's more, Lou Myers's adorable illustrations also remind us that cooking (and, of course, eating) is one of life's great pleasures.

A historian by trade and a humanitarian by nature, Edda continues to be a gift to the Jewish world and, for all of us, a living testament to the over 2,000-year legacy of Italian Jewry.

Joan Nathan

PREFACE

THE IDEA FOR A COOKBOOK SOLELY DEVOTED to Jewish desserts came to me while I was engaged in doing research for my first cookbook, THE CLASSIC CUISINE OF THE ITALIAN JEWS. Whenever I interviewed an elderly Italian Jew for authentic ancient recipes, the first item that she (more often a she but occasionally also a he) offered me was a dessert, whether it was some kind of biscotti, a cake, preserves, candied fruit, or a syrup. But back then I was interested only in general recipes: I had accumulated enough dessert recipes from my parents and relatives that I really didn't need any more of them. But I recorded them nevertheless, partly to show appreciation for the people's generosity in sharing their precious heirlooms with me, and partly... Well, just in case. Eventually the number of general recipes I was able to gather was large enough to fill a second cookbook, which I called THE CLASSIC CUISINE OF THE ITALIAN JEWS II. But even with a second book, there was a large number of dessert recipes that remained unpublished.

As it turned out, my two cookbooks contained more—and more intriguing—dessert recipes than any other Italian cookbook I knew of. This brought me back to the original idea of an all-dessert cookbook, and led me to speculate that if I added recipes from other Jewish cultures as well, I would certainly come up with a sizable and valuable volume.

However, at that time, in addition to compiling, testing and writing recipes for my second cookbook and enriching it, as I had done with my first one, with anecdotes and some of my most remarkable childhood experiences, I was involved in coordinating my notes and wartime journals for a strictly memoir book—one, that is, that would not deal with recipes at all. This turned out to be a most difficult task. Not only did it stir so many different emotions that sometimes I didn't know where or who I was, lost in the confusing labyrinth of conscious and unconscious, present and past, narrow paths constantly meeting and separating, and often found myself screaming wildly as I was sitting in front of my typewriter, scaring the wits out of my young children; but it also made me face the actual, the present, the real and practical problem of having to be selective in order not to come out with a *War-and-Peace*-length tome.

So, to preserve my sanity, I decided that for the time being, I would put both projects—the dessert book and the memoir one—on the back burner, and totally dedicated myself to finishing the second cookbook. When this task was accomplished, I corrected and revised my first book, and called it, THE CLASSIC CUISINE OF THE ITALIAN JEWS I. Now that I had this successful pair happily flying all over the world, the time had come for me to resume my other two projects. But although a third book that dealt in recipes might have seemed the logical path to follow, I gave the memoir precedence over the dessert book because the approach of the fifthieth anniversary of the liberation of Europe awakened me to the reality that it would be now or never. So stimulated, I began the painful and lengthy process of writing my memoir. Many years had intervened since I had first made an attempt at putting my life of that period down on paper, and I acknowledged with relief to myself that I had become emotionally better equipped to deal with digging up again the difficult past.

Now that also this book—CHILD OF THE GHETTO, *Coming of Age in Fascist Italy, A Memoir, 1926-1946*—has been in print for a while and has a life of its own, here I am again implementing my old idea of a Jewish dessert cookbook.

In a sense I am happy that I have waited this long to write such a book. Since the time that this idea first popped into my head, the tastes of Americans have gone through many phases. All in all, I have observed that people have become more sophisticated, more accepting of new and different food ideas, and especially more than ever enamoured of exotic fare. I remember the first time I offered a very wealthy and supposedly sophisticated lady a Campari-and-soda drink. She made a wry face and said, "How can you drink this stuff? It tastes like medicine!" Or when the word *mascarpone* was so new and alien that few people could even pronounce it, much less use it. Now I hardly know anybody who doesn't talk about Campari, *mascarpone, penne al basilico, tiramisu,* and other by-most-people-hitherto-unknown foods and drinks—with authority.

Then, of course, as in any other aspects of life, there are fashions and fads. But now the dialectical pendulum of what's acceptable and "good" food, begins its swing back. For example, until recently, the word "fat" was the bugbear of the culinary vocabulary. Too much fat is bad for one's health to be sure; but so is too much salt, too much sugar, too much wine, too much bread, too much of any "good" thing...

Fat is necessary for our survival, as are salt and sugar. Use of butter, in fact, is now on the rise again, and so is the use of sugar and salt—in moderation, of course. As I have mentioned time and again in my other two books, when foods are prepared in good taste and are therefore satisfying, people have less need and less desire to eat in oversized quantities. This, for sure, also holds true for desserts.

Some time ago, I read an article in a reputable scientific magazine that chocolate, the quintessential "bad guy" of foods, is actually good for people who have high cholesterol, since it contains the antioxidant that "protects LDLs—the so-called bad lipoproteins—from oxidation." (Science News: October 12, 1996, vol. 150, page 135.)

It is said that sweets numb our taste buds, stopping us from craving more food. I don't know how scientifically proven this is, but it is a fact that in our civilization we have chosen to put *dulcis in fundo,* the sweet at the end of the meal.

Sweets at the end of a meal—whether presented as a simple dish of fresh fruits or as an elaborate, rich, sugary dessert—have become standard in the cuisines of most cultures (even though I am aware that many people use some form of sweet in soups, in main dishes, in vegetables, in salads, and even straight at the beginning of a meal). The cuisine of the Jews is no exception.

Jews, more than most people of other cultures, have traditionally prepared their own desserts, even when—as is the case in Italy—the store-bought ones can be, and often are, not only better presented visually, but also better tasting than anything that is made at home. There are two reasons why Jews have always prepared their own desserts. The first and foremost is—at least for those who strictly adhere to it—the observance of their dietary laws. The multimillion-dollar kosher-food industry of today is a relatively young business. However, before this kosher-food boom—and certainly outside of the United States where until recently there was no obligation to list the ingredients—Jews who observe kashrut were not at liberty to buy their desserts. Whereas other people could choose to make *or* to buy their desserts, the observant Jews had no such a choice—if they wanted to be sure that no non-kosher ingredients were included in their preparations—but to make their own.

The second reason gives Jewish desserts a unique and folkloristic dimension. Having been chosen by the rest of humanity as the target against which to satisfy its need for aggressiveness and destructiveness, Jews have experienced, throughout their history, more than their share of persecutions from their fellow humans. This unconscionable reality has brought about much pain and misery, needless to say. In order to counteract, and, in some superstitious minds, to ward off such obnoxious and unwarranted behavior toward them, the Jews have resorted to preparing their own special desserts to sweeten up a little their otherwise embittered and miserable existences. Even in times of relative tranquillity, desserts that symbolize their past tribulations are prepared and served on special occasions, but only when there is a happy ending to the historical event. For example, the mortar the Jews of antiquity were forced to toil with to build Pharaoh's pyramids became the sweet charoset used for the Passover Seder and throughout the remaining eight days of this celebration of freedom. Hamantachen, at Purim, mimic the tripointed hat supposedly worn by their vicious persecutor Haman of biblical notoriety. Latkes, or pancakes fried in oil, traditionally eaten during the eight days of Chanukkah, remind us of the victory over the Syrian army of Antiochus Epiphanes by the Maccabee brothers, and the miracle of the oil. Chanukkah lasts eight days to celebrate this miracle in which one days worth of consecrated and undefiled oil, that was used to feed the eternal light inside the sanctuary, lasted eight days, the time needed to prepare and consecrate a new supply of oil.

Jewish women have always vied with each other in preparing more and more diverse types of desserts. And with the passing of time, the two reasons the Jews had for making their own sweets have given rise to a multitude of varied and delightful desserts among which are those that surpass their store-bought counterparts and, many of which are, as mentioned above, symbolic reminders of past tribulations—and victories.

I chose to give this collection the subtitle "A World of Jewish Desserts," not only because metaphorically the expression "a world of" stands for "a great number of," but also because, in a literal sense, some of these desserts come from various parts of the world, kindly passed along to me by people whose background is different from mine.

I give prominence to Italian desserts for the obvious reason that I have first-hand experience with them; but also and above all because I have come to realize, through feedback from my enthusiastic readers and fans, that Italian Jewish food in general, and desserts in particular, are favorites among a great number of people—whether they are of Jewish descent or from different cultures altogether.

****

For practical purposes I have organized this collection in the alphabetic order of their Italian titles. Next to each recipe I have indicated whether the dessert is to be used only with a dairy meal (D), or whether it can be used with both a dairy or a meat-based meal

(P), pareve. You will know also from the indexes under which category a dessert falls.

The indexes will also indicate which dessert is traditionally served on a given holiday. For example, *ceciarchiata,* the bits of pasta and nuts glued together by cooked honey, also known as *taighlach*, will appear under Rosh-Hashanah, under Purim, and even under Passover desserts. The latter is made possible by preparing it with matza meal in place of flour, and in this case it qualifies as "kosher for Pesach."

Preparing desserts is a very satisfying endeavor. Parents should get into the habit of encouraging children to help make desserts. Not only are a few extra pairs of helping hands really needed to speed up operations, but also the process gives the very young children a feeling of self-worth, and the not so young ones less time to get into trouble.

I hope with this collection to give people the same pleasure that—according to the many users of my cookbooks who have repeatedly let me know—I have given them with my first two.

Enjoy and live it up!

Edda Servi Machlin
Croton-on-Hudson, NY
June 1999

THE RIGHT INGREDIENTS

Nowadays finding the right ingredients, even the most exotic ones, is no longer the problem it was when, over two decades ago, I embarked on the writing of my first recipe book. However, some are still hard or even impossible to find in America, and one has to resort to substituting ingredients that are only somewhat similar to the original ones. A good example is vanilla bean crystals. If vanilla crystals are available where you live, by all means use them even though the recipe calls for vanilla extract. Extracts are never as strongly aromatic as crystals because they are diluted in alcohol, water, or other liquids. Therefore, when I give directions for 1 teaspoon vanilla extract, for example, you only need a tiny pinch (something like 1/16 of a teaspoon) of crystals to obtain the same (or better) result. Vanilla beans, on the other hand, can be readily found and enhance certain recipes, but cannot be used for certain others.

Some of the original recipes called for bitter almonds, which cannot be found commercially (and cracking the shells of such hard pits might prove too difficult and time-consuming). So my directions call for almond extract, which is in fact derived from the bitter almonds of peach pits and sometimes of apricot pits.

Many desserts require the flavoring of zest, the grated rind of a lemon or an orange. By all means make your own fresh zest whenever you can, because the dry version commercially available has lost most of its original aroma. All you need is a lemon or an orange, both of which should never be lacking from your fruit bowl. You can grate the rind directly from the whole fruit or peel it off thinly and then cut it with a very sharp knife into tiny pieces. If you have a small coffee grinder, you can use it to grind the rind and make your own fresh lemon or orange zest (a food processor or a large coffee grinder would not work). In either case, make sure to exclude from the rind the pith of the fruit which does not have any flavor and adds unwanted heaviness to your dessert.

Oftentimes Americans call "anise" the white knob of the fennel, confusing thus two altogether different plants: fennel, or *finocchio*, a native of Eurasia, and anise, a native of the countries bordering the Mediterranean Sea. The seeds of the former are somewhat larger and lighter in color than the anise seeds, and are used in stuffings, in stews and other “salty” dishes. The tiny darker seeds of the anise plant, also called aniseeds, are strongly scented, and are used in medicine as well as for flavoring in baking. Even though the appearance and aroma of the two may seem similar to an untrained palate or sense of smell, to my taste buds and olfaction, they are quite distinct. I most certainly would not use them interchangeably.

During World War II, when I was sheltered by some courageous and generous Italian farmers I saw ricotta being made and made it myself many times. Sheep milk, after being curdled, was brought to a boil and the casein separated from the whey and gathered into a form to become the delicious *pecorino* (from *pecora,* the Italian word for sheep). After the cheese was removed, the whey was brought again to a boil and from this doubly boiled liquid the white ricotta rose to the surface. The word *ricotta*, in fact, means cooked twice.

Italians make great use of ricotta in their desserts. Although "ricotta cheese" is readily available in any supermarket, it is not equivalent to Italian ricotta just described. For certain dishes, such as ravioli, I have found that *ricotta salata,* which can be found in many specialty food shops, is perfectly adequate. However, for desserts we have to resort to the commercial ricotta cheese as a substitute. But, it cannot be used as it comes from the container. To give it the desired consistency, leave it in a shallow pan over a very low heat, stirring occasionally, for at least 1/2 hour and preferably for 1 hour.

It is not rare that my dessert recipes call for olive oil. There are two basic reasons for this. One is that when margarine did not yet exist or was rarely found in the old countries, oil was used in place of butter in order for the dessert to be pareve, or equally suitable for any meal, including one based on meat. Italian as well as other Mediterranean Jews, have traditionally used olive oil, which was probably the only cooking oil available to them. (I remember that when I was a child there were only two types of vegetable oil, in addition to the medicinal ones, commercially available: linseed oil, as a base for painting and as a furniture polish, and olive oil, which was the only commestible one. A slice of Tuscan bread with some salt and oil was often our *merenda*, a midday snack, and to date I still cherish the very same snack.) The other reason is that even if they had access to other vegetable oils, they simply preferred the taste of olive oil in their desserts. However, many people, especially those of Eastern-European origin, do not like the strong flavor that olive oil can sometimes have, so I suggest that they use whatever vegetable oil they favor. And if olive oil is indeed a favorite, it is advisable to use the refined one, rather than the extra virgin type which, although perfect for enhancing the taste of any raw salad and many cooked dishes, would definitely detract from the delicate flavor of a dessert.

I rarely call for butter, but when I do it is always the unsalted type, since the salted one might not be as fresh. In fact, I buy only 1 pound at a time, divided into 4 sticks individually wrapped in foil, and keep in the freezer what I don't use immediately. If I become ambitious and find the time, I make my own fresh butter. And if you really want to know what fresh butter tastes like, you ought to make a little yourself. Buy the freshest of heavy cream you can find. Whip it in a small bowl at high speed until it forms stiff peaks, then decrease the speed and continue beating until the butter separates from the milk. Strain the tasty milk and save it for later use (in coffee, in cereal, etc.). Gather the butter into a ball, and run cold water over it until the water appears clear. Store in refrigerator, in a bowl with icy water until you are ready to use it. But remember that, having no preservatives, it does not stay fresh for very long. When we were children and milk was not homogenized, we let it rest until all the cream had come to the surface, and then we gathered it into a glass and beat it with a teaspoon to make our own delicious butter.

Although occasionally recipes might call for cake flour (which is lighter than all-purpose flour), and during Passover we must use Passover cake flour, I generally prefer to use unbleached flour, which is the most natural one, aside from the stone-ground whole-wheat flour. Any flour (but especially so whole-wheat flour and corn meal) is highly perishable. Even when you don't see mould or detect a foul odor, the flavor may have lost its original goodness. I therefore suggest that you buy small batches (1, 2, up to 5-pound bags at most) and that in between uses you keep them in the refrigerator or, better yet, in the freezer.

Alkermes, a liquor widely used in Italy in bakery and especially for *Zuppa Inglese* for its delicate flavor and bright-red color, is not available in America, or at least I have not been able to locate it. You may use in its place any red liqueur (since color is a main appeal), mixed with your favorite extract (anise, vanilla, almond, chocolate, etc.), or with a mixture of extracts, since the original Alkermes is flavored with many different aromas.

Wines are often used in desserts (*Bruscadella, Charoset* and *Zabaione* come first to mind), but I don't recommend any particular ones since many good kosher wines are available on the American market. I limit myself to suggesting whether it should be sweet or dry.

To conclude, it is possible that by the time you read this you will be able to find the exact ingredients recommended for your desserts. But if this proves to be a problem, read my suggestions and put your imagination to work to create the substitutes that best approach the original.

Le Ricette

RECIPES

A

AGNOLOTTI DOLCI
SWEET TORTELLINI (P)

2 cups unbleached flour
1/2 teaspoon salt
1/4 cup sugar
2 eggs
Olive oil or other vegetable oil you favor
2 tablespoons rum or brandy
1 teaspoon freshly grated lemon rind
3/4 cup thick jam or preserve you favor
Vanilla-flavored sugar (page 234)

Make a soft dough with flour, salt, sugar, eggs, 3 tablespoons oil, rum and lemon zest. Knead for three minutes, then cover with a clean towel and let rest for 5 minutes. With a rolling pin or a manual pasta machine, roll the dough thin.

With a cookie cutter or a small glass, cut disks 1 1/2 to 2 inches in diameter. Place a scant teaspoon of preserve over each disk. Fold each disk in half and press the round edge with a fork to seal. Heat a cup of oil and fry the *agnolotti* until golden. Drain on paper towel. Serve piping hot sprinkled with vanilla-flavored confectioners sugar.

Yields about 4 dozen.

AMARETTI DI SARONNO
SARONNO ALMOND COOKIES (P)

In Italy we used to make *amaretti,* whose name literally means, "small bitters," with the very bitter almonds of peach pits. In America I use regular almonds with almond extract which, according to its list of ingredients, is made from "bitter almonds." These cookies are a favorite at Purim and during Passover.

3 egg whites
Dash salt
1 cup granulated sugar
3 teaspoons almond extract
1/2 teaspoon vanilla extract
1 1/2 cups finely ground blanched almonds
2 tablespoons pareve margarine or oil

Beat the egg whites with salt until stiff, gradually adding sugar, and almond and vanilla extracts. Add the finely ground almonds and gently mix.

Lightly grease a baking sheet and cover with baking paper. Drop the almond mixture by the rounded teaspoonful, holding the spoon perpendicular to the sheet in order to make round little mounds.

Bake in preheated 350 °F oven for 20 minutes or until *amaretti* are lightly browned.

Yields 2 to 3 dozen.

APERE DI PESACH
PASSOVER COOKIES (P)

Bruno D'Angeli, a dear old friend from Venice, Italy, gave me this recipe for cookies that are traditionally made for Passover, they are so light and delightful that you will want to have them at hand any time of the year.

5 eggs
1 1/2 cups sugar
1 teaspoon anise extract
1 teaspoon freshly grated lemon rind
2 cups Passover cake flour

Beat eggs with sugar, anise extract and lemon rind. Gradually add enough flour to form a not too loose batter.

Spoon over a non-stick baking sheet, holding the spoon vertically to obtain round medallions. Bake in preheated 300 °F oven for 10 minutes, or until cookies are lightly golden. Let cool on baking sheet at room temperature before storing in a clean white pillow case.

Yields approximately 48.

APPLE BLINTZES
APPLE-FILLED CREPES (P)

2 eggs, slightly beaten
Pinch salt
3/4 cup orange juice
1 1/2 cups pareve margarine, melted
1/4 cup unbleached flour
2 large cooking apples, peeled, cored and chopped
1/2 cup blanched almonds, chopped fine
1 teaspoon cinnamon
1 1/2 tablespoons sugar
Vanilla-flavored sugar (page 234)

Mix together without excessive beating (since a somewhat lumpy batter makes for lighter crepes) eggs, salt, orange juice, 1/4 cup margarine, and flour. Brush a 7-inch skillet with margarine and place on moderate heat. Pour 2 or 3 tablespoons batter into the hot skillet and tilt it to spread the batter evenly. Cook just until the crepe is barely firm. Turn upside down over a lightly damp cloth. Repeat until you have batter, brushing the skillet with margarine as it becomes necessary and turning the crepes over the cloth in single layer.

Mix together apples, almonds, cinnamon, and sugar. Spread one tablespoon of apple mixture close to one edge of the crepes. Starting from the side nearest to the filling, make one fold over it. Turn a bit of the sides over the first fold, then finish rolling the crepe.

Just before serving, fry a few at a time in margarine, with seam side down first, then turning once, until golden on both sides. Draim on paper towel. Sift confectioners sugar over the blintzes and serve.

Serves 8.

ARANCE CANDITE
CANDIED ORANGES (P)

6 large seedless oranges
Water
Sugar
1 1/2 teaspoons vanilla extract

Place the oranges in a large bowl with plenty of cold water. Cover with an inverted dish slightly smaller than the bowl so that the oranges are under water at all times, and keep in refrigerator for 3 days.

Discard the water and weigh the drained oranges. Slice, unpealed, into long wedges, 1/4 to 1/2 inch thick at the largest point. Weigh the sugar to be half the weight of the oranges, and place both in a pot over moderately high heat with 1/4 cup water and the vanilla extract. Bring to a boil, stirring occasionally, then lower the heat and cook, uncovered, 45 minutes, or until wedges are in a thick sauce. Let cool thoroughly before storing in jars in the refrigerator.

Yields approximately 5 cups.

ARANCE LIQUORATE
ORANGES AU LIQUEUR (P)

It happens to everybody, once in a while, to have unexpected guests and no time to prepare one's favorite dessert. It happens to me quite often; but I always have lots of good fruit at hand; nuts in the freezer and baking chocolate on the baking shelf are also never missing. With very little time involved, I present my guests with an elegant and flavorful dessert.

6 large seedless oranges
1/4 cup sugar
1/4 cup pinoli *(Italian pine nuts), or any nuts you have at hand*
3 ounces semisweet chocolate
3/4 cup of your favorite liqueur

Peel the oranges and slice them into 4 or 5 slices each. Place in single layer, or slightly overlapping, on a serving dish. Sprinkle with sugar and pine nuts and set aside.

One moment before serving, grate the chocolate with a vegetable grater directly and evenly over the slices, pour the liqueur over all and serve, making sure that everyone gets some of the liquid.

Serves 6.

NOTE: If you happen to have kiwi fruits and/or strawberries, it enhances the look of your plate (and of course the taste of your dessert) if you top each orange slice with a slice or two of these colorful fruits.

ARANCINI
CHOCOLATE-COVERED ORANGE PEELS (P)

2 large, thick-skinned oranges
Water
2/3 cup sugar
1/4 cup light corn syrup
12 ounces semisweet baking chocolate, cut up
1 tablespoon margarine

Remove the two "poles" from oranges and make a few cuts lengthwise to separate the peel from the pulp. Reserve the fruit for the orange jelly of page 113.

Cut the peels into slim strips (about 24 per orange), place in a container with fresh water and keep in refrigerator for 3 full days.

Drain and place peels in a saucepan covered with fresh water and bring to a boil. Cook for about 15 minutes then drain. Place in a skillet with sugar, syrup, and 2 tablespoons water. Bring to a boil and cook on moderately high heat, uncovered, until almost dry—approximately 30 minutes. Lower heat and stir until syrup is quite dense. Turn the peels out on a piece of wax paper and allow to cool thoroughly.

Dissolve the chocolate and margarine in a heavy-bottomed saucepan over very low heat, stirring constantly, then remove from heat. Keep on stirring for a few minutes, then quickly dip each peel into it, and line on sheets of wax paper. Gently reheat chocolate if it becomes too hard and keep on stirring and coating. Let rest at room temperature until coating has solidified (several hours or overnight) before peeling off wax paper and storing in a cookie jar.

Yields approximately 4 dozen.

AZZIME DOLCI ALL'UOVO

SWEET EGG MATZOT (P)

In my village *azzime*, matzot, were made in the community oven in the days that preceded Passover. Together with the plain matzot, we made a number of different sweets, among which figured prominently the matzot of the following two recipes.

2 eggs
3/4 cup sugar
1 teaspoon salt
1/2 cup olive oil
3 tablespoons dry vermouth
2 teaspoons anise seeds
1 teaspoon grated lemon rind
3 cups Passover cake flour

Beat together eggs, sugar, and salt. Add the oil, vermouth, anise seeds, and lemon zest and mix well. Gradually add the flour until a soft dough is formed. Turn out on an oiled work surface and knead until dough is smooth and elastic.

With your hands roll into a 6-inch-long cylinder, then cut the cylinder into 6 equal round slices. With an oiled rolling pin, roll each disk down to 1/4-inch thickness. Pinch two concentric circular rows of holes this way: lift the disk on one side, and pinch tightly, 1/4-inch from the border, with your thumb and forefinger, making two holes. Move the forefinger into the hole made by the thumb (toward you) and pinch another hole. Continue all around until the first loop of holes is completed. Now make another loop of holes inside the first one, and repeat for the other disks.

Arrange on an oiled and floured baking sheet, and bake in preheated 450 °F oven for 15 minutes, or until matzot are golden brown.

Yields 6.

AZZIME DOLCI AL VINO
SWEET WINE MATZOT (P)

2 1/2 cups Passover cake flour
1/2 cup sugar
1/2 cup olive oil
1/2 cup dry white wine
2 teaspoons anise seeds
1 teaspoon salt

Combine all the ingredients in a bowl and form a dough. Turn out over an oiled surface and knead until smooth and elastic.

With your hands roll into a 6-inch-long cylinder; then cut into 6 equal round slices. With an oiled rolling pin, roll each disk down to 1/4-inch thickness. Pinch two concentric rows of holes (see preceding recipe for this technique) and arrange on a lightly oiled and well flowered baking sheet.

Bake in 450 °F oven for 15 minutes. Serve as a wholesome snack or breakfast food.

Yields 6

BACI DI CIOCCOLATA
CHOCOLATE KISSES (D)

1/2 pound plus 48 hazelnuts or filberts
8 ounces finest milk chocolate, coarsely chopped
3 teaspoons vanilla extract
1 1/2 pounds semisweet baking chocolate
1 tablespoon butter

Toast all the nuts until the peels are black. As soon as can be handled peel them by rubbing a few at a time between the palms of your hands. Choose 48 of the largests nuts and put them aside. Chop the remaining nuts fine, but be careful not to pulverize them.

In a heavy-bottomed pan, over low heat, place the milk chocolate and 2 teaspoons vanilla extract and stir until chocolate is barely melted. Remove from heat, add chopped nuts and mix well.

Turn out over a sheet of wax paper, cover with another sheet and with a rolling pin or the palms of your hands, flatten down to approximately 3/4 inch thickness. Let cool for a while, then peel off the top sheet and cut the solidified chocolate into 48 small squares.

With your fingers round off the side corners of each square to shape them into rounded, somewhat conical mounds, as you line them up over a fresh piece of wax paper.

Place 8 ounces of semisweet chocolate into a clean heavy-bottomed small pan, stir over very low heat until completely melted, then remove from heat. Take the whole nuts one by one, smear with melted chocolate, and place on top of each little mound (the melted chocolate should act as adhesive). Let cool for at least two hours. Reheat the melted chocolate.

Holding with prongs or your fingers, quickly dip the bottoms of each mound 1/4 inch deep into the melted chocolate, and return to waxed paper, freshly-coated-side down. Let rest for at least 2 hours.

Melt the remaining 16 ounces of semisweet chocolate with the butter and, holding the mounds upside down, dip them into the melted chocolate and return them upside up to wax paper to solidify. Leave at room temperature one whole day before storing in cookie jars at room temperature, where "kisses" remain fresh for several weeks.

It is a long process and you might want to make it into a project to carry out with your [older] children, but the reward is unbelievably worth while.

Yields 4 dozen.

BAKLAVA
A RICH MIDDLE EAST PASTRY (P OR D)

Baklava had not made it to Italy while I was living there, and I tasted it for the first time in 1981 in Detroit when, following the publication of my first book, I was invited at the Jewish Book Fair to give a talk on the Italian Jewry and its cuisine. The lecture was a true success: few people, if any, had even heard about the very existence of the Italian Jews, much less of their cuisine! After the talk, I was treated to a dinner at a Greek Jewish restaurant. For dessert I chose baklava and at the moment I believed it to be only a Greek dessert. Eventually I found out that the Jews of Syria also make it, and so do other Jews of the Middle East. It varies slightly from country to country, and from kitchen to kitchen, but it is always a rich, satisfying dessert. Here is my own version.

2 cups sugar
1/2 cup water
1/4 cup honey
1 pound frozen filo dough (20 sheets), defrosted according to manufacturer's directions
1/2 pound pareve margarine or unsalted butter, melted with 1/4 cup olive oil
2 cups walnut meats, chopped neither coarse nor too fine
1 cup pecan meats, chopped as above
2 teaspoons ground cinnamon
1/2 teaspoon ground cloves
Dash or two grated nutmeg
Grated rind of 1 medium orange

Prepare a syrup by placing 1 3/4 cups sugar and 1/2 cup water in a saucepan; bring it to a boil and gently cook for 15 minutes. Add the honey and cook for another 5 minutes. Remove from heat and let stand at room temperature.

Keep the defrosted filo dough covered with a slightly damp cloth, so that the sheets do not become dry and brittle.

Brush the bottom and sides of a 13 x 18 x 2 inches baking pan with the melted margarine/oil mixture. Place one sheet of filo at the bottom of the pan and lightly grease it with the mixture. Repeat the procedure another 4 times.

Combine the chopped nuts with cinnamon, clove, nutmeg, orange zest, and 1/4 cup sugar. Spread 1/3 of the nut mixture evenly over the stack of filo sheets, then cover with another 5 sheets, brushing each one of them with the mixture. Spread another third of the nuts and cover them with 5 sheets of filo, brushing, as before, each sheet. Spread the final third of the nuts and drizzle a few teaspoons of syrup over it before covering it with the last 5 sheets, always brushing each with the margarine mixture, then brush also the top.

With a pizza cutter or a very sharp knife, score the top diagonally and vertically to form approximately 48 diamonds. Bake in 350 °F oven for 45 minutes or until the top is golden.

Remove from the oven and cut the diamonds all the way through. Immediately pour all the syrup evenly over the hot baklava and leave at room temperature until ready to serve.

Serves 12 or more.

NOTE: Baklava does not need refrigeration for several weeks, and it tastes better if made a few days in advance.

BIANCHI MANGIA'

ALMOND TURNOVERS (D OR P)

My mother never made this typical Roman Jewish dessert (at least not since I was old enough to remember, and by then she had 5 children and little time for complicated desserts), because making the prescribed flaky dough was a little too lengthy, and she could make outstanding desserts which required less laborious preparations. Also, being fanatic about our health habits, she shunned away as much as she could from fried food. Like most Italian women of the time, she did not have an oven in her kitchen. But as a child in Rome, she had enjoyed this dessert at the homes of wealthy relatives, and she often talked to us about it with a tinge of warm nostalgia. When I became a housewife myself here in America, I discovered that I could easily make *Bianchi Mangia'* with filo dough, so I was finally able to taste this famous Roman dessert. Today we can choose to fry or to bake *Bianchi*. However, like my mother, I prefer the baked version.

2 cups blanched almonds,finely chopped
1 cup sugar
1 egg, slightly beaten
2 tablespoons finely chopped candied citron peel
1 tablespoon grated lemon rind
8 sheets frozen filo dough, defrosted according to manufacturer's directions
1/4 cup butter or non dairy margarine, melted
3 tablespoons olive oil
Vanilla-flavored sugar (page 234)

Mix together almonds, sugar, egg, citron peel and lemon zest in a small bowl and set aside.

Delicately unfold the filo dough over a clean surface, keeping it covered with a slightly damp cloth, so that it does not become dry and brittle. Mix together butter and oil and brush a thin film of this mixture over each sheet of filo, except for the top one. With a round pastry cutter or wine glass, approximately 3 1/2 inches in diameter, cut 12 discs.

Place one twelfth of the filling over each disk, fold in half and seal the edges tight, moistening them with water and pressing firmly down. With the prongs of a fork, practice a few holes on the tops.

Place on an ungreased baking sheet, and bake in a preheated 450 °F oven for 15 minutes or until only lightly golden. Remove from oven and immediately dust with confectioners sugar.

Yields 12.

BISCOTTI ALLA MANDORLA PER PESACH

PASSOVER ALMOND BISCOTTI (P)

The word "biscotti" in Italy has come to designate all sorts of hard cookies. But in reality this word was originally coined for what nowadays, in America, is appropriately called "biscotti." In fact "bis" derives from Latin and means "once more, twice," and "cotti" is the Italian word for cooked, baked. Therefore, biscotti are called thus because they are cooked twice.

Although the classic, the typical, the "authentic" biscotti Mamma prepared for the eight days of Pesach were the *anisette* of the recipe following this one, occasionally also almond biscotti were made for Passover. They differ in taste and texture, but they were both winners in my parents' household in Italy as they are in my American home.

1 1/3 cups sugar
1/2 teaspoon salt
1/3 cup olive oil
3 eggs
3 1/2 cups Passover cake flour
1 cup whole unblanched almonds
2 teaspoons almond extract
1 teaspoon vanilla extract

Cream together sugar and oil. Add eggs, one at a time, beating after each addition. Add almonds, almond extract, and vanilla extract. Add enough flour to make a rather soft but manageable dough.

Pour over an oiled work surface and divide into three parts. Oil your hands and shape into 3 cylinders 15 inches long. Place on a lightly oiled and floured baking sheet and bake in 350 °F oven for 30 minutes or until tops are golden.

Remove from oven (move the rack to the top shelf and raise the temperature to 450 °F) and as soon as can be handled, cut diagonally to obtain approximately 60 slices, 1/2 to 3/4-inch thick. Line up on the baking sheet resting on a cut side and bake on the top rack for 10 minutes, or until toasted on both sides.

Cool thoroughly on cooling rack before storing. I would suggest not to store in an air-tight bag or jar, nor in the refrigerator, but, as my mother did—and I still do—to place them into a clean linen pillow case at room temperature and they will remain crisp for the eight days of Passover.

Yields approximately 5 dozen.

BISCOTTI DELLA MAMMA PER PESACH

MAMMA'S ANISETTES FOR PASSOVER (P)

1 1/3 cups sugar
1/2 teaspoon salt
1/3 cup olive oil
3 eggs
2 tablespoons anise seeds
1/4 cup anisette liquor
1 teaspoon vanilla extract
3 1/2 cups Passover cake flour

Cream together sugar, salt and oil. Add eggs, one at a time, beating after each addition. Add anise seeds, anisette liquor and vanilla extract. Add enough flour to make a rather soft but manageable dough.

Turn out over an oiled work surface, and divide into three parts. Oil your hands and shape into 3 cylinders 15 inches long. Place on a lightly oiled and floured baking sheet and bake in a 350 °F oven for 25 minutes or until tops are golden.

Remove from oven (move the rack to the top shelf and raise the oven temperature to 450 °F) and cut diagonally to make approximately 60 slices, 1/2 to 3/4-inch thick. Line up on the baking sheet resting on a cut side and bake on the top rack for 10 minutes or until nicely toasted on both sides.

Cool thoroughly on cooling rack before storing. (See the preceding recipe for my suggestion; Mamma used to store the pillow cases filled with biscotti inside the prepared-for-Pesach credenza together with the freshly-made matzot.)

Yields 4 to 5 dozen.

BISCOTTINI DI NOCI

WALNUT COOKIES (P)

1 pound walnut meats
1 1/4 cups unbleached flour
2 eggs

Place the walnuts in a food processor and process for 8 seconds. Transfer to a mixing bowl; add flour, eggs, sugar, honey, orange zest, chocolate chips, and margarine and mix well to combine.

Take 1 tablespoonful at a time, and make 24 mounds over an ungreased non-stick baking sheet 2 inches apart. Lightly flatten down and bake in preheated 325 °F oven for 12 minutes. Cool on rack.

1 3/4 cups sugar
1 tablespoon honey
1 teaspoon freshly grated orange rind
1/2 cup semisweet chocolate chips
4 tablespoons pareve margarine, melted

Yields 24.

BISCOTTINI PRATESI
PRATO LITTLE BISCOTTI (P)

Prato, the small town in the outskirts of Florence, owes its claim to fame more to its textile industry than to its food. These almond biscotti, however, give Prato a good name also in the dolciaria industry. They are not suited for Passover, as are the almond biscotti described above, but they have the advantage of containing no eggs, and are therefore desirable for people who watch their cholesterol intake.

1/4 cup olive oil
1 cup sugar
1/2 teaspoon salt
2 teaspoons almond extract
1 cup whole unblanched almonds
1 teaspoon vanilla extract
1/2 cup dry white wine or water
3 teaspoons baking powder
3 cups unbleached flour

In a large bowl, place all the ingredients except for the baking powder and flour. Mix with a fork or wooden spatula. Sift together 3 teaspoons of baking powder and two cups of the flour over the bowl and mix thoroughly. Add enough flour to obtain a rather stiff dough.

Spread the remaining flour on a work surface, and turn out the dough over it. Divide into four parts and knead each, squeezing with your hands for a compact dough. Roll into 16-inch-long ropes, and place on an ungreased non-stick baking sheet. Flatten the ropes to 1/4-inch thickness, and bake in 375 °F oven for 20 minutes.

Remove from oven and as soon as can be handled, cut diagonally into 1/2-inch slices. Place on the baking sheet resting on a cut side, and bake again for 15 minutes, or until golden brown.

Remove to a cooling rack and wait until thoroughly cool before storing in a cookie jar.

Yields approximately 5 dozen.

BISCOTTINI DI RONA
RONA'S VANILLA COOKIES (P)

As I have mentioned elsewhere, biscotti (or biscottini, when they are small) designate in Italy any kind of hard cookies. These cookies were devised by my daughter Rona when she was a little child: she told me what ingredients should go into making them and I took care of the amounts and measurements of those ingredients. She not only liked them for herself, but also and above all to offer them to her little friends when they took a break from their play at tea time.

3/4 cup firmly packed raw sugar
1/2 cup olive oil
1/4 teaspoon salt
2 eggs
2 teaspoons vanilla extract
1 1/4 cups unbleached flour

In a small bowl, cream together sugar, oil and salt. Add one egg at a time, beating after each addition. Add vanilla and beat again. Gradually add flour and continue to beat until you have a smooth batter.

Drop by the teaspoonful (holding the spoon perpendicular to the sheet to obtain rounder cookies) on a lightly oiled and dusted with flour baking sheet, 2 inches apart. Bake in preheated 375 °F oven for 7 minutes or until cookies are slightly browned. Cool thoroughly before storing in cooking jar.

Yields about 3 dozen.

BISSE PER PESACH
S-SHAPED PASSOVER COOKIES (P)

1 1/2 cups sugar
1/4 cup olive oil
5 eggs
2 cups Passover cake flour
1 teaspoon anise extract
1 teaspoon freshly grated lemon rind

Beat sugar and oil. Add eggs, one at a time, beating after each addition. Gradually add flour, anise extract and lemon zest.

Fill a pastry bag with the mixture and squeeze small amounts over a greased and floured baking sheet, giving the cookies the shape of esses. Bake in preheated 300 °F oven for 7 to 10 minutes, or until cookies are lightly golden. Let cool on sheet at room temperature before storing in cookie jar.

Yields approximately 48.

BOCCA DI DAMA PER PESACH
LADY'S MOUTH FOR PASSOVER (P)

4 eggs, separated
3/4 cup sugar
1 cup blanched almonds, chopped fine
1 teaspoon grated lemon rind
2 tablespoons potato starch
3 tablespoons pareve margarine
2 tablespoons fine matza meal

Beat the egg whites until stiff and dry. In a separate bowl, beat the yolks with sugar until lemon colored. Add the almonds, lemon zest, and potato starch and beat to mix. Gently fold in the beaten egg whites.

Pour into an 8-inch springform cake pan, well greased with margarine and dusted with matza meal. Bake in preheated 300 °F oven for 1/2 hour. Turn the oven off and let the cake rest inside with the door ajar for 15 minutes. Let cool at room temperature before unmolding.

Serves 6.

BOLLO
YOM KIPPUR BREAD (P)

Bollo, in some parts of Italy, is prepared as a Sukkot bread; in others it is made as a Shabbat bread, or Challa. In our community it was traditionally made around Rosh-Hashanah and was used to break the fast—accompanied by a small glass of sweet vermouth—at the end of Yom Kippur.

5 1/2 cups unbleached flour
2 envelopes active dry yeast
1 teaspoon sugar
1 cup warm water
3 eggs
1 1/4 cups sugar
1/2 cup olive oil
2 tablespoons anise seeds (optional)
2 teaspoons vanilla extract
2 teaspoons salt
1 teaspoon grated lemon rind
1 small egg beaten with a small pinch of salt

Have all the ingredients at room temperature. Combine 1 1/2 cups of flour with dry yeast, 1 teaspoon sugar, and 1 cup of warm water in a large bowl. Beat until you have a very smooth soft dough. Lightly sprinkle the top with flour, cover with a damp warm towel, and set aside in a warm place for about 2 hours, or until more than doubled in bulk.

Add the eggs and sugar and begin to beat. Scald the oil with the anise seeds and add to the bowl, while beating. Add vanilla extract, salt, and lemon zest. Gradually add enough flour to make a soft dough.

Spread the remaining flour on a work surface. Turn out the content of the bowl over it, and knead, gathering flour, until you have a dough that is stiff enough to hold its shape. Divide into two equal parts, knead 2 minutes, and let rest 5 minutes. Shape each part into a 12-inch-long oval loaf and place on a lightly oiled and generously floured baking sheet.

Cover with a towel and let rise in a warm place for 1 to 2 hours, or until doubled. Brush the tops with the beaten egg, and place in preheated 450 °F oven. Immediately lower the heat to 350 °F and bake 30 minutes or until dark brown.

Yields 2 1-pound loaves.

BOMBA DI RISO GIA
GIA'S RICE AND PRESERVE OMELET (D)

1 1/4 cups Italian rice
1 1/2 cups cold water
1 cup milk
1 teaspoon salt
2 tablespoons sugar
1 teaspoon grated lemon rind
1 teaspoon vanilla extract
4 eggs, slightly beaten
3 tablespoons vegetable oil
3/4 cup fruit preserves

Place rice in a saucepan with water, milk, salt and sugar. Bring to a boil over moderate heat; reduce heat and simmer, covered for another 15 minutes. Remove from heat, add lemon zest and vanilla extract and stir for a couple of minutes to cool. Add the beaten eggs and mix well.

In a large frying pan, heat 2 tablespoons of oil; pour half the rice mixture and immediately lower the heat to its lowest point. Spread all the preserves over the rice (leave 1/2 inch margin all around), then cover with the remaining rice mixture.

Cook over the lowest heat until a golden crust is formed at the bottom, shaking the pan occasionally to make sure that the mixture is not sticking to the pan. The whole process should not take more than 15 minutes.

Turn the *bomba* by placing an inverted dish over the pan. With one hand holding the pan and the other hand over the dish, turn pan and dish at the same time. Heat the remaining oil in the pan and carefully slide the omelet into it. Cook over the lowest heat for 5 minutes or until all egg is cooked through, and the other side is golden brown. Serve warm or at room temperature.

Serves 6.

NOTE: The method described above to turn a large omelet is actually very simple, but for an unexperienced cook it might take a bit of practice. Another way of cooking *bomba* is to pour half the rice mixture in an oiled 10-inch cake pan, add the preserves, the remaining rice mixture and a drizzle of oil, and bake in 375 °F oven for 45 minutes.

BOMBOLONI RIPIENI

JELLY DOUGHNUTS (P)

1 package active dry yeast
1 500 mg vitamin C, pulverized
1/4 cup warm water
Sugar
Pinch salt
2 egg yolks
Olive oil
Grated rind of 1 lemon
2 cups unbleached flour
1 cup jam or preserve

Dissolve the yeast and the vitamin C in a mixing bowl with the warm water, 1 tablespoon sugar and the salt, and let rest 5 minutes.

Add the egg yolks, 2 tablespoons sugar, 2 tablespoons olive oil, and the lemon zest and beat well. Add 1 cup flour, beat well again, then cover the bowl with plastic wrap and let rest for 20 minutes.

Mound the remaining flour over a work surface, make a depression at center and turn out the batter in it. Knead, gathering flour, to make a rather soft, elastic dough. Cover with a clean towel and let rest in a cool place for several hours or overnight.

Punch down, divide into 24, and make a ball out of each portion. Cover and let rise again for 1/2 hour. Delicately insert a teaspoon of jam inside each ball and make sure to close the opening well so that no leaking occurs during frying.

Heat enough oil in a saucepan to stand 2 1/2 inches deep and fry a few *bomboloni* at a time in it until golden on all sides. Drain on paper towel. When they are all done, roll them in sugar and serve hot or, for convenience, at room temperature.

Yields 24.

BORRICCHE PITIGLIANESI
CINNAMON TURNOVER (P)

1 1/2 cups sugar
2 tablespoons powdered cinnamon
2 tablespoons brandy
2 tablespoons water
Double amount of the flaky dough from page 172
1 egg beaten with 1 pinch salt

Combine sugar, cinnamon, brandy, and water and mix to obtain a paste.

Roll the prepared flaky dough down to approximately 1/8-inch thickness, trying to avoid tears. With a very sharp knife or a pizza cutter, cut into 12 squares.

Spread 1 heaping tablespoon of sugar mixture over half the square diagonally (on one triangle), leaving one inch free along the edges. Wet the edge with some of the beaten egg.

Starting from the corner with the filling, loosely roll up the pastry, pinching the sides closed to prevent sugar from escaping during baking. With a sharp pointy knife poke a few cuts here and there to allow the hot steam to escape while baking, then lightly brush the tops with the beaten egg.

Line up on an ungreased baking sheet and bake in preheated 400 °F oven for 15 minutes. Serve at room temperature.

Yields 12.

BORRICCHE ALLA CANNELLA

CINNAMON TURNOVER II (P)

The authentic *Borricche* we used to make for Purim, are those of the preceding recipe, prepared with homemade flaky dough. Now I can buy Kosher filo dough practically in any supermarket, and the preparation of *borricche* is no longer the lengthy process it used to be. Filo dough is much more delicate than the homemade flaky dough, and now I like *borricche* even better than the original ones.

3/4 cup sugar
1 1/2 tablespoons powdered cinnamon
2 tablespoons brandy
8 12x18-inch sheets of filo dough, defrosted according to manufacturer's directions
1/4 cup olive oil
1 egg beaten with a pinch of salt

Sift together sugar and cinnamon into a small bowl. Add the brandy and mix with a spoon until most of the mixture is slightly moist.

Delicately unfold the filo dough over a clean surface. Brush a thin film of oil over each sheet, stacking the sheet back together. With a sharp knife or pizza cutter, divide across the length into two, and make two cuts widthwise to form 6 squares.

Spread one sixth of the sugar mixture over each square, covering only one triangle, and leaving 1 inch free along the edges. Starting from the corner of the triangle with the mixture, roll each *borricca* and close it tightly by moistening with water (using a clean brush, not the oily one) the openings and pressing firmly with your fingers. With a sharp pointy knife poke a few slots on the tops to allow steam to escape while baking.

Brush the tops with the beaten egg, line up on an ungreased baking sheet, and place in preheated 425 °F oven for 7 minutes.

Yields 6.

BORRICCHE ALLE NOCI
WALNUT TURNOVER (P)

1/3 cup honey
1/4 teaspoon cinnamon
1/8 teaspoon ground cloves
Dash ground nutmeg
2 teaspoons freshly grated orange rind
3/4 cup finely chopped walnut meats
Flaky dough from page 172
1 egg beaten with a pinch of salt

Place honey, cinnamon, cloves, and nutmeg in a skillet over moderately high heat. Bring to a boil and cook 2 minutes. Add orange zest and walnuts and cook another 3 minutes, stirring constantly. Remove from heat, keep on stirring for a couple of minutes, then set aside to cool.

Roll the flaky dough down to approximately 1/8-inch thickness. Cut into 6 squares with a sharp knife or pizza cutter.

Spread 1/6 of filling over each square diagonally, covering only one triangle and leaving 1 inch free along the edges. Moisten the edges with some of the beaten egg. Starting from the corner with the filling, roll up the pastry and pinch the sides closed to prevent the filling from escaping during baking. With a sharp pointy knife poke a few slots on the tops to allow hot steam to escape. Lightly brush the tops with the beaten egg.

Line up on an ungreased cookie sheet and place in preheated 375 °F oven for 15 minutes. Serve at room temperature.

Yields 6

BRUSCADELLA DI KIPPUR

YOM KIPPUR BRUSCADELLA (P)

In different parts of Italy people have different ways of breaking the fast of Yom Kippur. This simple yet delicious *bruscadella* was kindly given to me by Dr. Lucetta Jarach Guastalla who lives in Turin, Piedmont.

12 slices of stale, hearty bread
1 cup sugar, mixed with 1 tablespoon cinnamon
1 pint dry red wine

Toast the slices of bread dark and arrange them in layers in a souffle dish, sprinkling each layer abundantly with the sugar/cinnamon mixture. Pour all the wine over the bread, and let rest a few minutes before serving.

Serves 6.

BRUTTI E BUONI

UGLY AND GOOD (P)

1 cup sugar
4 teaspoons baking powder
3 egg whites
Small pinch salt
1/2 cup unsweetened cocoa
1 cup hazel nuts or filberts
Grated rind of 1 orange

Combine sugar and baking powder in a measuring cup with a spout. Beat the egg whites with salt until stiff and dry. Gradually pour in the sugar mixture and continue beating until stiff peaks form. Add cocoa, nuts, and orange zest and mix to combine.

Lightly grease a cookie sheet and line it with baking paper. Drop the mixture over it by the teaspoonful about 2 inches apart. Bake in preheated 225 °F oven for 20 minutes.

Yields about 4 dozen.

BUDINO ALL'ARANCIA
ORANGE PUDDING (P)

1 large seedless orange, unpeeled
1/4 cup blanched almonds
2 teaspoons almond extract
1 1/4 cups sugar
3 eggs
1 egg yolk
1/3 cup orange juice
12 lady fingers, coarsely cut up

Boil the orange in water until very soft, about 30 minutes. Drain and let cool at room temperature. In the work bowl of a food processor fitted with the metal blade, place the almonds and process 10 seconds. Add almond extract, 1/2 cup sugar, whole eggs and egg yolk and process 10 more seconds. Cut up the orange, add to the bowl and process until quite mashed. Add orange juice and lady fingers and process until you have a homogeneous batter.

Cook the remaining 3/4 cup sugar with 2 teaspoons water in a 1 1/2-quart pudding mold until melted and honey-colored. Remove from heat and tilt the mold to coat also part of the sides.

Pour the orange batter into the mold and place this in a shallow pan with 2 inches of hot water. Bake in preheated 350 °F oven for 1 hour or until a skewer inserted into the center comes out somewhat clean. Remove from oven and let cool at room temperature, covered with a piece of wax paper. Loosen the sides and invert over a serving dish.

Serves 6.

BUDINO AL CIOCCOLATO
CHOCOLATE PUDDING (D)

3 1/2 cups milk, hot
3 ounces semisweet baking chocolate, cut into small chunks
Sugar
8 lady fingers, pulverized in a food processor
1 teaspoon vanilla extract
4 eggs, slightly beaten
2 tablespoons unsalted butter, soft

Place 1/2 cup hot milk and the chocolate in a saucepan over low heat and stir until the chocolate is melted. Slowly add the remaining hot milk, and 1/2 cup sugar, and simmer, stirring, 5 minutes. Add the pulverized lady fingers and simmer 5 more minutes.

Remove from heat, add vanilla extract, stir, and let cool at room temperature. Add the beaten eggs and mix. Pour into a 1 1/2-quart mold, buttered and dusted with sugar. Place the mold inside a larger pan filled to the level of the chocolate mixture with hot water and let simmer on a low heat for 1 hour and 15 minutes. Remove from the bain-marie, let cool for a while, then unmold and serve.

Serves 6.

BUDINO AL LIMONE
LEMON PUDDING (P)

1 whole lemon
2 cups sugar
2 eggs
6 egg yolks
The juice of 4 lemons
1/2 cup water
1 tablespoon rum

Keep the whole lemon in fresh water for 3 full days. Bring the water with the lemon to a full boil, then lower the heat and simmer for 1 1/2 hours. Drain, cool and cut the lemon open to remove any seeds. Place in a food processor and process until liquefied.

Cook 1 cup sugar with a few drops of water until melted and dark-honey colored. Pour into an oval oven-resistant 1 1/2 quart container. Tilt the container to completely coat the bottom and part of the sides.

Beat the eggs and egg yolks with 1 cup of sugar until frothy and lemon colored. Gradually add the liquefied lemon, the lemon juice, the water and rum. Pour into the oval container and place this in a shallow pan with 1/2 inch of hot water. Cover with a piece of wax paper.

Bake in 350 °F oven for 30 to 45 minutes or until a straw inserted at center comes out clean. Let rest at room temperature for a few hours. Run the blade of a knife to separate the custard from the container walls then invert over an oval serving plate.

Serves 6.

BUDINO DI CIOCCOLATA PER PESACH

PASSOVER CHOCOLATE PUDDING (P)

7 eggs, separated
Small pinch salt
1 1/3 cups sugar
1 teaspoon vanilla extract
Freshly grated rind of 1 orange
1/4 cup orange juice
1/3 cup unsweetened cocoa
1/3 cup potato starch
Vanilla-flavored sugar (page 234)

Beat the egg whites with salt until stiff peaks form and set aside. Beat the egg yolks with sugar, vanilla extract, orange zest and orange juice until frothy and lemon colored. Sift together cocoa and potato starch and add gradually to the bowl, mixing well. Add one third of the beaten egg whites and mix to soften the batter. Fold in the remaining egg whites, then spoon the batter into an ungreased tube pan with removable bottom.

Bake in preheated 350 °F oven for 45 minutes or until a skewer inserted in the highest point comes out clean. Remove from oven and invert over a cooling rack. When cooled to room temperature, run the blade of a knife all around the mold and invert over a serving plate. Sprinkle with vanilla-flavored confectioners sugar.

Serves 12.

BUDINO DI MANDORLE
ALMOND PUDDING (D)

10 ounces blanched almonds
4 eggs
2 egg yolks
1 1/2 cups sugar
1 teaspoon almond extract
1 cup whipping cream
2 tablespoons vanilla-flavored sugar (page 234)

Toast the almonds dark under the broiler or in the microwave oven. Cool a little, then chop very fine.

Beat the eggs and egg yolks with 1 cup sugar until frothy and lemon colored. Gradually add the toasted almonds and almond extract.

Heat the remaining 1/2 cup sugar with a few drops of water in a 1 1/2-quart pudding mold until melted and slightly colored. Remove from heat and tilt the mold a little to spread the sugar on part of the sides. Spoon the almond mixture into it and place in a shallow pan with 2 inches of warm water. Bake in 350 °F oven for 45 minutes or until a skewer inserted at center comes out clean. Cool at room temperature covered with a piece of wax paper. Loosen the sides and invert over a serving dish. Beat the cream until soft peaks form; mix in the confectioners sugar, then spoon over the pudding and serve.

Serves 6.

BUDINO DI PANE
BREAD PUDDING (P)

5 eggs, separated
pinch salt
1 1/2 cups sugar
1 cup plain bread crumbs
Freshly grated rind of 1 lemon
1 teaspoon vanilla extract

Beat the egg whites with salt until stiff and dry. In a clean bowl, beat the egg yolks with 1 cup sugar until frothy and lemon colored. Gradually add the bread crumbs, lemon zest and vanilla extract.

Place the remaining 1/2 cup sugar with a few drops of water in a 1 1/2-quart pudding mold and cook until melted and slightly colored. Remove from heat and tilt the mold to coat also part of the sides. Delicately fold the beaten whites in the bread batter, then spoon into the mold.

Place in a shallow pan with 2 inches of hot water and bake in 350 °F oven for 45 minutes, or until a skewer inserted at center comes out clean. Cool at room temperature, covered with a piece of wax paper.

Loosen the sides and invert over a dish and serve.

Serves 6.

BUDINO DI RISO ALL'ITALIANA

RICE PUDDING ITALIAN STYLE (D)

1/2 cup Italian rice
Unsalted butter
2 cups milk, warm
1/2 teaspoon salt
1/3 cup sugar
2 tablespoons finely chopped candied citron peel
Grated rind of 1 lemon
1 teaspoon vanilla extract
1 egg
1 egg yolk
1/2 cup all-purpose flour, sifted with 1 teaspoon baking powder
Fine plain bread crumbs
Vanilla-flavored sugar (page 234)

Place rice with 2 tablespoons butter in a heavy-bottomed saucepan over low heat. Stir until the butter is melted and rice is all coated. Add milk and slowly bring to a gentle simmer. Lower heat to a minimum and cook without stirring, covered, 20 minutes, or until rice is well done and moisture almost completely gone.

Remove from heat and add sugar, citron peel, lemon zest, and vanilla extract. Stir until mixture is somewhat cooled, then add egg, egg yolk, flour/baking powder mixture and mix to combine.

Generously butter and sprinkle with fine bread crumbs a 1 1/2-quart pudding mold. Spoon the mixture into it and bake in preheated 350 °F oven for 45 minutes, or until a skewer inserted at center comes out clean. Unmold over a serving plate and lightly sprinkle with vanilla-flavored confectioners sugar. Serve hot, or, for convenience, at room temperature.

Serves 6.

BUDINO DI RISO ALLA TURCA
TURKISH RICE PUDDING (D)

1 1/2 cups milk
1/2 cup water
1/2 teaspoon salt
1/2 cup sugar
1 cup rice
Grated rind of 1 lemon
Cinnamon

Place milk and water in a saucepan with salt and slowly bring to a boil. Add sugar and rice and cook over low heat, stirring frequently to prevent sticking to bottom, for 10 minutes. Add lemon zest and cook 10 minutes longer, or until rice is well done. Serve at room temperature sprinkled with cinnamon.

Serves 6.

BUDINO DI RISO EDDA
EDDA'S RICE PUDDING (D)

Although I like rice in any form or shape, none of the various rice puddings I had tasted were good enough for my palate. And as I mentioned time and again, when a food is not satisfying, one tends to eat more of it in the vane search of gratification. So I made up my own version of this pudding, a small amount of which is sufficient to make me happy.

4 tablespoons unsalted butter
1 cup Italian or short-grain rice
3 cups milk
1/2 teaspoon salt
2 tablespoons flour
1 cup sugar
1/2 cup raisins
2 teaspoons vanilla extract
1 egg, slightly beaten

Place 2 tablespoons butter in a saucepan over moderately high heat with the rice, and stir until rice is all coated. Add 2 1/2 cups milk and salt and bring to a gentle simmer. Reduce the heat to minimum, cover the pan and let cook for 20-25 minutes, stirring occasionally. Remove from heat.

In a large skillet melt 2 tablespoons butter with 2 tablespoons flour. Add the remaining 1/2 cup of milk and stir constantly over moderate heat until thickened and smooth. Add sugar, raisins, vanilla extract, and beaten egg and cook, stirring, 5 more minutes. Remove from heat, add the rice and stir to combine. Let cool for a while then add rum and lemon zest and mix. Spoon into flute glasses and refrigerate until ready to serve. Serve as is or topped by whipped cream.

Serves 12.

2 tablespoons rum
2 teaspoons freshly grated lemon rind
Whipped cream (optional)

BUDINO MOKA

CHOCOLATE-COFFEE PUDDING (D)

Mix lady-finger crumbs and coffee and set aside for a while. Beat the egg whites with salt until stiff peaks form. In a clean bowl beat the yolks with sugar, then add the coffee mixture, cocoa, 1/4 cup butter, and vanilla extract and mix well. Fold in the egg whites.

Butter a 1 1/2-quart pudding mold and spoon the mixture into it. Place inside a pan with hot water not to exceed the level of the batter. Bring the water to a gentle boil, and let the pudding simmer in the bain-marie for 1 1/4 hours. Remove from heat and after a few minutes loosen the sides, unmold and serve, as is or with English Cream.

Serves 6.

1/4 cup lady fingers, crushed into crumbs
1/2 cup very strong espresso coffee
4 eggs, separated
Small pinch salt
3/4 cup sugar
1 cup sifted unsweetened cocoa
1/4 cup plus 2 tablespoons unsalted butter, melted
1 teaspoon vanilla extract
English Cream (page 83), optional

CASSATA SICILIANA
SICILIAN RICOTTA CAKE (D)

1 pint whole-milk ricotta
1 cup sugar
1/2 cup semisweet chocolate chips
30 lady fingers
1/2 cup Marsala wine
3 egg whites
3/4 cup vanilla-flavored sugar (page 234)
1 tablespoon lemon juice
Arancini (page 33)
1/2 cup mixed candied fruit

Beat together ricotta and sugar until creamy and light. Add chocolate chips and stir to combine.

Line the bottom of a 10-inch shallow souffle dish with half the lady fingers and sprinkle with half the Marsala. Spread the ricotta mixture over them. Cover with the remaining lady fingers and sprinkle with the remaining Marsala.

Beat the egg whites stiff. Add the vanilla-flavored sugar and lemon juice and beat just to combine. Cook in a double-boiler, stirring constantly, until the mixture begins to thicken—3 to 4 minutes. Pour over the cake and flatten evenly with a spatula. Garnish with *arancini* and candied fruit arranged to look like flowers, and refrigerate until ready to serve.

Serves 6.

CASSOLA ROMANA
OLD ROMAN RICOTTA FRITTATA (D)

1 Pound whole-milk ricotta
1 cup sugar
5 eggs
1/4 cup unbleached flour
Grated rind of 1 orange
5 tablespoons olive oil
Cinnamon sugar (optional)

Beat the ricotta with sugar until smooth. Add the eggs, one at a time, beating after each addition. Gradually add the flour and the orange zest, and mix well.

Heat 3 tablespoons of oil in a 10-inch skillet or iron frying pan. Spoon the mixture into the hot oil, flatten with a spatula, then lower the heat to minimum. Cook slowly, covered, shaking the skillet once in a while to make sure that the mixture does not stick to the bottom. When the bottom feels firm, remove from heat.

Invert a large dish over the skillet and turn the skillet while holding the dish, so that the omelet falls onto the dish. Return the skillet to the low heat, add the remaining oil, and slide the cassola into it. Cook until the other side is also firm.

Serve warm as is or topped with cinnamon sugar.

Serves 6 to 12.

NOTE: The above is the original Roman cassola. If you are not dexterous with turning omelets, pour the batter into a buttered-and-dusted-with- flour 10-inch springform cake pan and bake in 350 °F oven for 45 minutes or until a skewer inserted at center comes out somewhat clean.

CASTAGNE
CHESTNUTS (P)

When I first came to this country some forty years ago, fresh chestnuts were rather a rarity in the New York area. Now they have become more popular and every supermarket carries them during their short season - around Thanksgiving. Dried chestnuts, however, can be found throughout the year in most Italian grocery stores. Although the dried chestnuts are not quite as versatile as the fresh ones, they have the definite advantage of being almost entirely peeled and of being there at any time you need them.

Powdered chestnut, or chestnut flour, can also be found in Italian grocery stores. Keep it in a tightly closed jar in refrigerator, or even in the freezer, if you intend to keep it for more than a month. Always sift it before using, to loosen up lumps and also eliminate debris if there is any.

When you buy fresh chestnuts, be sure to choose the large, healthy ones without blemishes or holes - sure signs of their being rotten or beginning to spoil. Remember that a rotten chestnut gives a bad taste to all of the others when cooked together.

The following are the basic ways of preparing chestnuts and chestnut flour. In other parts of this volume you will find more sophisticated ways of preparing desserts with them.

BALLOTTE
BOILED CHESTNUTS (P)

This is the simplest way of cooking chestnuts. They are fun to eat as they are, and they are also the ones most used in the preparation of delightful desserts.

2 Pounds fresh chestnuts (4-6 dozen)
1 tablespoon salt
Water

Place the chestnuts in a saucepan with the salt and enough water to cover. Bring to a boil, then reduce heat and simmer, covered, for 45 minutes.

With a sharp knife cut each chestnut in half, not quite going through the bottom, so that the halves remain attached to one another. Serve immediately and let each person scoop out the pulp with a small spoon or a dull butter knife.

Serves 6.

MONDINE
PEELED BOILED CHESTNUTS (P)

2 Pounds fresh chestnuts (4-6 dozen)
1 teaspoon fennel seeds
2 teaspoons salt

Remove the outer, dark-brown shell from chestnuts this way: pare the little hairy tip of each chestnut, then insert the tip of a sharp small and pointy knife between the shell and the meat, and cut down until the shell can be easily removed. Place shelled chestnuts in a saucepan with fennel and salt and enough water to cover. Bring to a boil, then simmer, covered, for 20 minutes, or until chestnuts are tender, but still firm.

Serve hot and let people take the final peel from their own chestnuts, since this is part of the fun of eating them.

Serves 6.

NOTE: If you make *mondine* to be used in a stuffing or to make a dessert, peel off the inner light-brown skin as soon as you can handle them, because after the chestnuts get cool it will be almost impossible to peel them successfully.

BRUCIATE
ROASTED CHESTNUTS (P)

These are by far the most fun of all the cooked chestnuts. When we were little children and walked over 2 miles to school, autumn morning could be really nasty, and frostbite was a common ailment among the school children. One way our mother tried to overcome this problem was to fill our coat pockets with *bruciate* just as we were about to leave the house. We would keep our mittened hands next to the hot chestnuts and arrive at school safe and warm. Later we would eat the chestnuts as a midmorning snack. Now, during my Autumn cooking classes I make *bruciate* every evening, as we all sit around the hearth chatting, because I haven't yet found anyone who doesn't like them.

2 pounds fresh chestnuts (4-6 dozen)
1 Long-handled chestnut pan or a baking sheet*

With a sharp knife make a gash on each chestnut deep enough to reach the meat, but not so deep that it splits the chestnut. This will prevent an explosion from air expansion while roasting.

If you have a fireplace, by all means roast the chestnuts in the long-handled pan in a single layer; wait until the coals are bright, then place the pan directly over the embers. Roast the chestnuts until they become charred, shaking the pan frequently to turn them.

If you don't have a fireplace, roast the chestnuts on a baking sheet under the broiler for 15 to 20 minutes, shaking the baking sheet occasionally.

Transfer the *bruciate* to a basket lined with a quilt or a kitchen towel folded many times, cover with another folded towel and serve immediately.

Serves 6.

* A Chestnut pan is a tin pan the bottom of which has been pierced with holes, much like a cheese grater.

CASTAGNACCIO

CHESTNUT PIE (P)

1 pound (about 3 cups) chestnut flour
3 1/2 cups cold water
1/3 cup pinoli *(Italian pine nuts)*
1/2 cup dark, seedless raisins
1 teaspoon salt
4 tablespoons olive oil
1/2 teaspoon rosemary leaves (optional)

Sift flour into a bowl. Gradually add 3 1/2 cups of cold water, stirring to prevent lumps from forming. Add pinoli, raisins, and salt and mix well to combine.

Pour into a well oiled baking pan in which the batter will stand 1/2 inch high. Sprinkle with the remaining oil and with rosemary leaves.

Bake in preheated 375 °F oven for 45 minutes to 1 hour, or until lightly browned and top is all cracked.

Serves 6 or more.

CASTAGNE SECCHE

DRIED CHESTNUTS (P)

Sometimes you might want to try a recipe that calls for *mondine* but cannot find fresh chestnuts. You might then try the recipe with dried chestnuts. Before you cook them, inspect them very carefully, because if even one rotten chestnut remains in the bunch, all will take on a bad taste.

1 1/2 pounds dried chestnuts
1/4 teaspoon salt
1/2 teaspoons anise seeds or fennel seeds
6 cups hot water.

Discard any chestnuts that are obviously spoiled. Rinse the remaining ones in warm water, then place in a saucepan with salt, anise seeds (if you use them for a dessert) or fennel seeds (if they are for poultry stuffing) and 6 cups of hot water. Bring to a boil, then reduce the heat and simmer, covered, 3/4 hour. Drain.

If you find that bits of peel are still on, it is easy to remove them at this point, using the tip of a sharp knife. Use *castagne secche* thus prepared in place of *mondine*.

Yields approximately 3 1/2 cups.

CASTAGNOLE DI PURIM

PURIM PETARDS (P)

Castagnola (the Italian for petard or fire cracker) is derived from *castagna*, chestnut. If chestnuts were to be roasted without the slit on the outer shell that allows hot air to escape, they would explode. Castagnole the sweet, however, will not explode if the frying oil is kept at a moderate temperature.

1 cup cake flour
Small pinch salt
1 teaspoon baking powder
3 tablespoons sugar
Freshly grated rind of 1 orange
1 teaspoon anise extract or vanilla extract
2 tablespoons olive oil
2 tablespoons brandy
1 egg
Vegetable oil for frying
Confectioners sugar
1 cup honey
1/4 cup water
1 tablespoon lemon juice

Combine flour, salt, baking powder, sugar, and orange zest. Add anise or vanilla extract, olive oil, brandy, and the egg and mix until you have a dough stiff enough to hold its shape. Roll into a rope slightly less than 1 inch thick, then cut into pieces slightly smaller than 1 inch. No need to shape into balls since they will become round as they fry.

In a small saucepan, heat 1 cup of oil to 375 °F on a deep-frying thermometer. Fry 8 or 9 pieces at a time, stirring with a fork to make sure they become golden on all sides. With a slotted spoon, transfer to a paper towel to drain.

Serve castagnole in either of these ways: 1) plain; 2) rolled in confectioners sugar; 3) in a honey syrup. To make the syrup, place honey, water and lemon juice in a saucepan and bring to a boil. Drop castagnole into the syrup, stir for 1 minute, then remove from heat. Serve warm or at room temperature.

Yields about 48.

CECIARCHIATA
TAIGLACH (P)

Ceciarchiata is one of the many sweets used for Purim and Rosh Hashana. It owes its name to the tiny pieces of dough in it, which resemble *ceci*, chick peas. I first discovered after I had come to America, that Jews of different background from mine also make it with slight variations. This is the authentic ancient recipe I learned to make as a child in Livorno from my mother's aristocratic sister, Aunt Letizia.

3 eggs, slightly beaten
2 cups unbleached flour
1/2 teaspoon salt
1 cup olive oil, optional
1 cup honey
1 cup hazel nuts
1 tablespoon lemon juice
2 teaspoons grated lemon rind
1 cup coarsely chopped toasted almonds

Combine eggs, flour and salt in a small bowl and mix to make a rather soft dough. Turn out on a floured surface and knead a minute or two. Shape into a ball, flatten down with your hands, then roll down to 1/4-inch thickness with a rolling pin, sprinkling with flour. With a sharp knife or pizza cutter, cut into 1/4-inch strips and dredge with flour. Cut a few strips at a time into pea-size bits, and again dredge with flour to prevent them from clumping together. Use a large sifter to remove excess flour.

If using the oil, heat it in a small sauce pan and fry a handfull of pasta bits at a time until golden. Drain on paper towel.

If you prefer to avoid fried food, forget the oil, and bake the bits, one third at a time, on an ungreased baking sheet in 400 °F oven for 7 minutes.

Bring the honey to a boil and cook over moderately high heat 3 minutes. Add the "chick peas," the hazel nuts, lemon juice and zest and cook over lower heat 7 minutes longer, stirring constantly.

Spread the toasted almonds over an oiled round dish and pour the hot mixture on it. Let settle for a few minutes. When the mixture is cool enough to handle, shape into a ring using your moistened hands and the help of a spoon. Let cool thoroughly at room temperature, then cut into 2-inch segments.

Serve 8 to 12.

CHAROSET ASHKENAZITA
GRANDMA'S CHAROSET (P)

Charoset is the symbolic food traditionally served as a dip during the Passover Seder(s) since it reminds us of the mortar the Jews of antiquity were forced to toil with in order to build Pharaoh's pyramids. In Pitigliano we made it with matza meal, wine vinegar and lots of sugar. Hardly a dessert. However, in other parts of Italy and of the world, charoset has become so elaborate and tasty that it is often served also as a delightful dessert. Of the many versions I am familiar with, I have chosen to share with my readers three: one from my husband's background (Ashkenazic), one of my own invention (Italian), and one from North Africa (Sefardic).

2 cups chopped unpeeled almonds
3 large apples, peeled, cored and chopped
1/2 cup red sweet wine
1/4 cup matza meal
1/2 cup honey

Mix together 1 cup of chopped almonds, apples, wine, matza meal and enough honey to form a consistent paste. Spread the remaining chopped almonds on a dish or a piece of wax paper. Make little balls of the apple mixture and roll them in the chopped almonds.

Serves 12.

CHAROSET EDDA

PASSOVER FRUIT AND NUT BALLS (P)

Charoset, the mortar-like paste used as a dip during the Passover Seder, comes in many versions and it is prepared as elaborately as people's imagination suggests. Mine is a favorite among family and friends not only as a dip, but also as a dessert.

1/2 pound pitted dates
1/2 pound walnut meats
3 large apples, cored and peeled
1 large whole seedless orange, unpeeled, washed
3 ripe large bananas
1/3 cup sweet Malaga wine
1/2 teaspoon cinnamon
1/8 teaspoon ground cloves
1 tablespoon lemon juice
Matza meal as needed
1/4 cup unsweetened cocoa
1/4 cup vanilla-flavored sugar (page 234)

Chop dates, walnuts, apples, and whole orange very fine and place in a bowl. Peel and mash bananas and add to the bowl. Add wine, cinnamon, cloves, and lemon juice and mix well. Add enough matza meal to make a mortar-like paste.

Mix together cocoa and confectioners sugar. Make little balls out of the paste and roll in the cocoa/sugar mixture.

Serves 12 to 20.

CHAROSET TRIPOLINA

CHAROSET FROM TRIPOLI (P)

2 tablespoons olive oil
1 pound pitted dates, coarsely chopped
1/4 cup seedless dark raisins
1/4 cup chopped walnuts
1/8 teaspoon nutmeg
1/8 teaspoon ground cloves
1/4 teaspoon ginger
1/4 teaspoon ground black pepper
1/4 cup wine vinegar

Heat the oil in a skillet then add all the other ingredients, except for the vinegar. Stir over moderate heat for 5 minutes, then remove from heat and let cool. Add the vinegar and mix to combine.

Serves 12.

CHEESE BLINTZES

CHEESE-FILLED CREPES (D)

1/2 cup unbleached flour
Pinch salt
3/4 cup milk
1/4 cup butter, melted
3 eggs, slightly beaten
Oil or butter for frying
1 pound farmer cheese, forced through a sieve
1 pint sour cream
1/4 cup sugar
1 teaspoon vanilla extract
1 teaspoon freshly grated lemon rind
Vanilla-flavored sugar (page 234)
1 Cup apple sauce or sour cream, optional

Mix together flour, salt and milk until smooth. Add butter and beaten eggs and beat just to mix. Brush a 7-inch skillet with oil or butter and place over moderate heat. Pour 2 or 3 tablespoons batter in the hot skillet, tilting it to distribute the batter evenly. Cook just until firm. Turn upside down over a lightly damp table cloth. Continue until you have batter, greasing the skillet as becomes necessary and turning the crepes over the cloth in a single layer.

Mix together cheese, 1/4 cup sour cream, sugar, vanilla extract, and lemon zest. Place one tablespoon of filling over each crepe close to one side. Starting with the side of the filling, fold the crepe once, fold a little of the two sides over the first fold, then finish rolling the crepe.

Just before serving, fry a few blintzes at a time in hot oil or butter, seam side down, turning once until golden on both sides. Drain on paper towel. Sift confectioners sugar over the hot blintzes and serve as are, or with a side dish of sour cream or apple sauce.

Serves 6.

CHEESECAKE
RICOTTA CAKE (D)

Cheesecake, the authentic rich fare, is not part of my repertoire. However, for Shavuot, I do make a cake that very much resembles the famous New York cheesecake, although the main ingredient is ricotta rather than cream cheese.

5 eggs, separated
Small pinch salt
1 cup sugar
1 pound ricotta, forced through a sieve
1/2 cup milk
3 tablespoons unbleached flour
2 teaspoons freshly grated orange rind
2 teaspoons vanilla extract
4 tablespoons butter, at room temperature
1/2 cup crumbed vanilla cookies
2 tablespoons brandy
1 teaspoon ground cinnamon
Vanilla-flavored sugar *(page 234)*

In a small bowl beat the egg whites with salt until stiff peaks form. In a larger bowl, beat together egg yolks and sugar until frothy and lemon colored. Reduce the speed and add the ricotta, 1/4 at a time, beating after each addition until mixture is smooth and silky. Slowly add the milk alternating it with the flour. Add the orange zest and vanilla extract, and lastly fold in the beaten egg whites.

With 2 tablespoons of butter, grease the sides of a 10-inch springform cake pan. Mix the remaining 2 tablespoons butter and the brandy with the crumbed cookies and flatten this mixture at the bottom of the cake pan. Spoon the ricotta mixture into it and bake in 325 °F oven for 1 hour without opening the oven door during baking.

Remove from oven and let cool at room temperature for several hours or overnight; then run a blade around the sides, remove the sides of the springform and transfer the cake to a serving dish. Sprinkle with vanilla-flavored confectioner's sugar.

Serves 8 to 12.

CIAMBELLINE DELLA ZIA DELIA PER PURIM
AUNT DELIA'S PURIM DOUGHNUTS (P)

Aunt Delia, like most housewifes in Italy before World War II, did not have an oven in her kitchen in Pisa, where she lived with her husband, the *chazan* of that community and her son, Rabbi Attilio Orvieto. Nor did she have easy access to a public oven, as we did in Pitigliano. Because of this, most of her specialties were fried. I have successfully converted many of her fried dishes into baked ones. For these delicious doughnuts, however, I give the authentic recipe as it was passed on to me.

2 1/2 cups unbleached flour
1 cup sugar
1/2 cup unsweetened cocoa
1 teaspoon baking soda
1/2 teaspoon salt
1/4 cup olive oil
4 eggs
1/2 cup finely chopped toasted almonds
1 teaspoon vanilla extract
Oil for frying
Vanilla-flavored sugar (page 202)

Sift 1 1/2 cups of flour with sugar, cocoa, baking soda, and salt in a large bowl. Add olive oil, eggs, almonds, and vanilla extract and beat at medium speed just until you have a homogeneous batter. Add enough of the remaining flour to form a soft dough. Turn out onto an oiled surface and quickly knead for a minute or so.

Divide into 24 or 30 pieces and shape each piece into a ball. With your thumbs and forefingers make a hole throught the center of each ball, stretching it and shaping it into a ring.

Heat enough oil in a small saucepan to be 3 inches deep. Fry one doughnut at a time for 1 minute on each side, turning only once. Transfer to a paper towel. Add oil to the pan as becomes necessary. When all doughnuts are done, roll them in vanilla-flavored sugar. Let cool thoroughly before serving.

Yields 2 to 2 1/2 dozen.

CIAMBELLONE
BREAKFAST RING (D)

1 cup sugar
1 stick (4 ounces) butter
3 eggs
1/2 cup seedless raisins
1/4 cup candied citron peel, diced
Grated rind of 1/2 lemon
1 teaspoon vanilla extract
4 1/2 cups unbleached flour
2 1/2 teaspoons baking powder
3/4 cup milk
1 egg, beaten with a small pinch of salt
1/2 cup blanched whole almonds

Cream together sugar and butter. Add eggs, one at a time, beating after each addition. Add raisins, candied citron peel, lemon zest, and vanilla extract and mix. Sift together 3 1/2 cups of flour and the baking powder and spread the remaining flour over a work surface. Add the flour mixture to the bowl alternating it with the milk.

Turn the content of the bowl over the floured surface, and quickly add enough flour to make a manageable but very soft dough. Shape into a ring and place on a greased and floured baking sheet. Lightly brush the top with beaten egg. Garnish with the whole almonds, then brush again the top over the almonds and on the sides with the remaining beaten egg.

Bake in 350 °F oven for 3/4 hour, or until a skewer inserted at the highest point of the ring comes out clean.

Serves 12 or more.

CIOCCOLATO IN TAZZA
HOT CHOCOLATE (D)

Hot chocolate in most parts of Italy is similar to what one gets in the United States. Very liquid and very sweet. And that's what we were treated with when we were children. However, once that I visited my brother Mario who's a professor at the University of Parma, I learned that there was another way to make *cioccolato in tazza.* To my surprise, the hot chocolate my brother offered me at his favorite caffè was not liquid, but as thick as a custard and it was to be enjoyed by "eating" it with a spoon.

1 cup heavy cream
1 tablespoon corn starch
1/2 cup sugar
3 1/2 cups milk
1 teaspoon vanilla extract
8 ounces semisweet baking chocolate, cut up

Whip the cream until soft peaks form and set aside. Dissolve the cornstarch and the sugar in 1/2 cup milk, add the vanilla extract and set aside.

Place the chocolate and 3 cups of milk in a heavy-bottomed saucepan and slowly heat, stirring constantly, until chocolate is completely melted. Add the milk mixture and bring to a gentle boil. Cook until thickened. Pour in cups, top with a tablespoon of whipped cream and serve before the cream has a chance to melt down.

Serves 6.

CONFETTURA DI FICHI

FRESH FIG CONFITURE (P)

Confettura di Fichi was a specialty of my cousin Bianca. Although she was a couple of years older than I, as children we were very close and spent a lot of time playing together, mostly making our own yarn dolls, knitting and crocheting their dresses and hats, or going to the woods to gather cyclamens. She got married and raised a family long before I did, and eventually we drifted apart. As a married woman in America each time I went to Italy and visited her, she made sure to present me with a little jar of this precious preserve. It never occur to me to ask her for the recipe, or maybe it did, but I refrained from doing so because I knew that it gave her a great deal of pleasure to make it for me. Now Bianca is no longer with us, and I can only guess at how she made it. Figs are seasonal and expensive, but if you find them during their short season—around Rosh-Ha-Shanah—by all means treat yourself. Figs come in black/purple and green. For this preserve you need to buy the green ones.

2 pounds small, ripe green figs
2 1/2 cups sugar
1/2 cup water
1/2 teaspoon grated lemon rind
3 tablespoons rum
1 teaspoon vanilla extract

Wash the figs thoroughly and, without peeling, cut them into small wedges. Place over moderate heat in a saucepan with sugar, water, and lemon zest. Bring to a boil and cook, stirring from time to time, until the syrup is dense and coats the spoon.

Remove from heat and let cool to room temperature. Add rum and vanilla extract, mix and store at room temperature or in refrigerator in a tightly closed glass jar.

Yields 4 cups.

CONFETTURA DI PESCHE

PEACH PRESERVE (P)

6 pounds firm, ripe peaches
3 cups sugar

Dip the peaches in boiling water for 1 minute, so that the peel will come off easily. Remove the stones and cut the pulp into small slivers.

Place in a heavy-bottomed saucepan and gently bring to a boil while stirring to prevent sticking to the bottom. Lower the heat to minimum, and simmer, covered, for 30 to 45 minutes, stirring occasionally.

Strain and reserve the liquid (2-3 cups) for the peach jelly of page 114.

Return the drained peaches to the saucepan, add the sugar and bring to a boil. Reduce the heat and cook uncovered, stirring occasionally, 30 minutes or until the wooden spoon comes out evenly coated with syrup.

Pour immediately into air-tight glass jars and wait until cool before storing in refrigerator.

Yields approximately 2 quarts.

CONFETTURA DI POMODORI
TOMATO PRESERVE (P)

You will want to make this preserve toward the end of summer, when tomatoes are plentiful and relatively inexpensive. Choose fruits that are very ripe but firm. Yellow tomatoes are ideal for this preserve, but red ones will also do well.

6 pounds ripe, firm tomatoes
1 1/2 pounds sugar
1 small lemon, quartered and seeded
1 teaspoon vanilla extract

Peel the tomatoes by dropping them in boiling water for a minute or two, then in cold water, and the peel will come off easily. Cut into chunks, remove as many seeds as you can, and drain most of the liquid out. You should be left with about 5 pounds.

Place tomatoes and sugar in a heavy-bottomed pot. Chop the lemon very fine, add it to the pot with the tomatoes and bring to a rapid boil. Lower the heat and simmer, uncovered, stirring occasionally with a wooden spoon, 1 hour or until a heavy syrup coats the spoon evenly.

Add the vanilla extract and stir. Remove from heat and almost immediately pour into air-tight glass jars. Wait until cool before storing in refrigerator.

Yields approximately 2 quarts.

COTOGNATA
SOLID QUINCE APPLE JAM (P)

4 pounds quince apples, washed in cold water
Water
1 stick cinnamon
3 whole cloves
Sugar

Peel and core the apples and place the peels and cores in a saucepan with 3 cups of water, cinnamon, and cloves and bring to a boil. Cook for 1/2 hour, then strain, discard solids and reserve the liquid.

Cut the peeled apples into thick slices, place in a pot

with the reserved liquid and add enough water to cover them completely. Gently cook until quite soft. Strain and reserve the water for *Gelatina* (page 113).

Puree the apples and measure the puree as you place it into a pan. Add 3/4 cup sugar for every cup of apple puree and cook on moderate heat for 3 to 4 hours, or until the jam has assumed a light maroon color.

Pour the jam into a 1 1/2-quart loaf pan, and cover with a piece of wax paper drenched in rum. Let it solidify at room temperature, where it preserves, without the need for refrigeration, for many weeks.

If everything went according to rules, you should have a solid jam that must be cut with a knife.

Yields approximately 1 1/2 quarts.

CREMA FRITTA

FRIED CREAM (D)

1/2 cup sugar
1/4 cup butter
Small pinch salt
Grated rind of 1 lemon
4 eggs
1 cup flour
2 cups milk
1 egg, slightly beaten
1 cup fine plain bread crumbs
Oil for frying
Vanilla-flavored sugar (page 234)

Cream together sugar, butter, salt, and lemon zest. Add 4 eggs, one at a time, beating after each addition. Lower the speed and add alternatively flour and milk.

Pour into a heavy-bottomed saucepan and cook on low heat, sitrring, until a dense cream is formed, about 7 minutes from when it starts bubbling.

Wet a flat surface or a large dish and pour the cream over it. With a wet spatula flatten down to 1/2-inch thickness. Let cool thoroughly. With the buttered blade of a sharp knife, cut into diamonds, dip in beaten egg, roll in bread crumbs and fry until golden on both sides. Dust with vanilla-flavored confectioners sugar and serve.

Serves 6.

CREMA INGLESE
ENGLISH CUSTARD (D)

In olden times in Italy all that was delicate and elegant was referred to as "English." (My mother used to call my older daughter *Inglesina*, little Englishwoman, because of her refined looks and manners.) This custard is called English as opposed to any other custard made with flour or other thickeners.

6 egg yolks
3/4 cup sugar
2 cups hot milk
1 teaspoon vanilla extract
Vanilla cookies or lady fingers

Beat egg yolks with sugar until frothy and lemon colored. Add the hot milk a little at a time, beating constantly.

Pour into a double-boiler or a heavy-bottomed saucepan and place over moderate heat. Cook stirring constantly with a wooden spoon until the cream coats the spoon evenly. (Be careful not to allow the cream to reach the boiling point.) Add vanilla extract, remove from heat and stir.

Cool to room temperature, stirring from time to time, then pour into individual custard cups and refrigerate. Serve with vanilla cookies or lady fingers.

Serves 6.

CREMA PASTICCERA
CUSTARD FILLING (D)

This type of custard is called *pasticcera* because it is used exclusively for pastry filling, or as part of a creamy dessert, such as *Tiramisu* and *Zuppa Inglese.*

4 egg yolks
2/3 cup sugar
Small pinch of salt

Beat the egg yolks, sugar and salt together until frothy and lemon colored. Gradually beat in the flour. Add the milk slowly and mix well. Pour into a heavy-bottomed

1/4 cup cake flour
2 1/2 cups hot milk
2 2 x 1/2 inches strips lemon peel
1 tablespoon unsalted butter

saucepan; add the lemon peel and place over moderately high heat. Bring to a gentle boil while stirring constantly. Lower the heat and simmer for 3 or 4 minutes, stirring occasionally.

Remove from heat, discard the lemon peel, add the butter, and stir. Cool for 1 to 2 hours, stirring from time to time to prevent a film from forming on the surface. If you don't use it right away, pour into a bowl and cover with a piece of wax paper, letting the paper touch the cream, then store in refrigerator.

Yields 2 to 2 1/2 cups.

NOTE: If you wish to use *crema pasticcera* for a Passover dessert, substitute Passover cake flour for the regular cake flour.

CRESPELLE CON CONFETTURE

SWEET CREPES WITH PRESERVES (P)

After the concentration camp situated in the province of Siena was dismantled toward the middle of June 1944, my parents and younger brother, who had been inmates there for 7 months, walked to the nearby village of Roccatederighi where my father knew a former customer from before the war. The man turned out to be the head of the fascist party and the owner of a luxurious hotel where he lived with his mother. In fear of the partisans and the Allies, the man and his mother fled leaving the three members of my family—fearful, emaciated, tired and nearly starved—to live there. A few days later, my older brother and I, after 7 days and 7 nights of incredible vicissitudes between the two fronts, were finally able to join them.

The very same day of our arrival, the hotel was requisitioned by the German Headquarters and we unwittingly hosted 5 high officers of the Weimar until the arrival of the Allies 5 days later. Although we would have liked to poison them, we treated them as if we were the fascist owners of the place, as they believed us to be. We had not seen sugar or other edible amenities for many, many years, but the cellar and the pantries of the hotel were full of every grace of God. It was then that I, barely 18, was appointed the "official cook." These crespelle became the favorite dessert of everyone, especially—needless to say—of the five of us who had not tasted such goodies in decades.

1/2 cup unbleached flour
Pinch of salt
3/4 cup water
2 tablespoons oil
3 eggs slightly beaten
2 tablespoon rum
Oil for frying
1 cup peach preserve (page 80)
Vanilla-flavored sugar (page 234)

Mix together flour, salt and water until smooth. Add 2 tablespoons oil, beaten eggs and rum and beat just to mix. Brush a 7-inch skillet with oil and place over moderate heat. Add 2 or 3 tablespoons of batter to the hot skillet, tilting it to distribute the batter evenly. Cook just until firm. Turn crepe and cook until firm on the other side. Continue until you have batter, turning the crepes over the table in stacks.

Spread one tablespoon of preserve over each crepe leaving a little margin all around, then roll. Place on a hot serving plate and sift confectioners sugar over them.

Serves 6.

CRESPELLE DOLCI

SWEET CREPES (D)

3/4 cup unbleached flour
Pinch salt
2 tablespoons sugar
1 cup milk
1/4 cup butter, melted
4 eggs slightly beaten
2 tablespoons rum
Butter for frying
Vanilla-flavored sugar (page 234)

Mix together flour, salt, sugar and milk until smooth. Add melted butter, beaten eggs rum and beat just to mix.

Brush a 7-inch skillet with butter and place over moderate heat. Add 2 or 3 tablespoons batter to the skillet, tilting it to distribute the batter evenly. Cook until firm. Turn crepe and cook until the other side is firm. Continue until no batter remains. Arrange on a large warm plate and sift confectioners sugar over crepes. Serve hot.

Serves 6.

CROCCANTINI ALLE MANDORLE

ALMOND CRUNCHIES (P)

3/4 cup sugar
2 tablespoons water
1/4 cup honey
1 1/2 cups whole, unpealed almonds
2 tablespoons oil

Place sugar and water in a medium skillet over high heat, and as soon as the sugar is dissolved add the honey. Lower the heat and cook, stirring occasionally, 7 minutes. Add the almonds and cook another 7 minutes, stirring occasionally. Remove from heat and keep on stirring until cooled a little—approximately 10 minutes.

Oil a large dish, cover it with aluminum foil, and sprinkle the foil with water. Spoon the almond mixture over the foil in little mounds and let cool thoroughly before peeling off the foil.

Yields about 12.

CROSTATA CON PASTA DI MANDORLE
PRESERVE PIE WITH ALMOND CRUST (D OR P)

Crostata in Italy is the name given to any torte, generally filled with a jam and topped with a lattice work made with part of the crust. The almond crust makes for a very rich dessert and it is more commonly used in the north of Italy. In Tuscany the crust mostly used for *crostate* is *pasta frolla,* as in the recipe following this one.

1 cup shelled almonds
1 cup sugar
1 cup unbleached flour
1 teaspoon powdered cinnamon
1/4 pound butter or non-dairy margarine, chilled
1 egg
2 egg yolks
1 1/2 cups orange, peach or strawberry preserves

Place almonds in a food processor fitted with the metal blade and process 10 seconds. Add sugar, cinnamon, and butter and process just enough to obtain a coarse meal. Do NOT overprocess.

Add egg and egg yolks and mix until all is moist. With 2/3 of the mixture line a 10-inch pie plate. Reserve a few pieces of preserve and spread the rest over the crust.

With the remaining crust mixture, make strips and form a lattice over the preserve. Garnish with the reserved pieces of preserve and bake in preheated 350 °F oven for 45 minutes.

Serves 12.

CROSTATA DI RICOTTA
RICOTTA PIE (D)

2 cups flour plus 2 tablespoons
1 cup sugar plus 3 tablespoons
10 tablespoons butter
5 eggs, separated
Grated rind of 1 lemon
1 1/4 cup warm milk
2 cups ricotta
1 teaspoon vanilla extract
1/4 cup candied orange peel, chopped fine
Small pinch salt
Vanilla-flavored sugar (page 234)

Make a dough with 2 cups flour, 3/4 cup sugar, butter, 3 egg yolks and grated lemon rind. Gather in a ball and place between two small dishes in the refrigerator for at least half hour.

Meanwhile make a cream. Beat 2 egg yolks with 3 tablespoons sugar; add 2 tablespoons flour, and gradually the warm milk, mixing well. Pour into a small saucepan and place over moderately high heat. Bring to a boil while stirring constantly. Lower the heat and simmer gently, stirring occasionally, for 3 minutes. Remove from heat and let cool for a while at room temperature.

Beat the ricotta with 1/4 cup sugar, slowly add the cream and the candied orange peel. Beat 4 egg whites until stiff peaks form, then fold in the ricotta mixture.

Take the crust dough from the refrigerator, divide into 3 parts, and place one back in the refrigerator. With the other 2 parts, make a ball. Roll down as thin as possible and line with it a lightly greased 10-inch pie dish. Pour the ricotta mixture into the crust. Take the remaining dough from the refrigerator and roll it very thin. Cut into 1-inch strips and form a lattice work over the ricotta.

Slightly beat the remaining egg white with a tiny pinch of salt and brush the top of the *crostata* with it. Bake in preheated 350 °F oven for 45 minutes. Remove from oven and sprinkle with vanilla-flavored confectioners sugar.

Serves 8.

CUSCUSSU' DOLCE
SWEET COUSCOUS (P)

Middle Eastern Jews brought coucous, a pasta product, to Italy where they have been preparing it in many different ways, including this delightful dessert. Sweet couscous is served on Tu B'Shvat, also called Rosh-Hashana Leilanot, the New Year of the Trees. It is customary for the Jews everywhere to celebrate Tu B'Shvat by eating all sorts of dry fruits and nuts, which are the main ingredients in this dessert. Regular couscous requires a tedious and proverbially-long preparation. However, for this dessert I successfully use the precooked type, thus cutting measurably the time of preparation.

2 1/2 cups water
1/2 teaspoon salt
2 tablespoons olive oil
3/4 pound precooked couscous
1/2 cup sugar
1 seedless whole orange unpeeled, washed and chopped fine
1/2 cup raisins
1/2 cup pitted dates, diced
1/2 cup blanched almonds, chopped
1/2 cup walnut meats, chopped
1 teaspoon cinnamon
1/2 teaspoon ground cloves
2 or 3 tablespoons fruit liqueur

Bring water with salt and olive oil to a boil. Add the couscous and stir. Cover the pot and remove from heat. After 5 minutes, add half the sugar and mix. Let cool at room temperature, fluffing it up with a fork from time to time.

Mix together fruits, nuts, spices and the remaining sugar in a serving bowl. Add the couscous, stirring to combine. Sprinkle with liqueur and serve.

Serves 6.

D

DICTINOBIS DI KIPPUR
DOUGHNUTS TO BREAK THE YOM KIPPUR FAST (P)

Whereas in Pitigliano we used *Bollo* to break the fast, in some parts of Italy *dictinobis* are used. They are an excellent holiday breakfast or midday snack.

2 envelopes active dry yeast
1/4 cup warm water
Sugar
1/2 cup confectioners sugar
1 1/2 cups unbleached flour
1/4 cup warm olive oil
2 teaspoons vanilla extract
1 jumbo egg
Oil for frying

Have all the ingredients at room temperature, except water and olive oil which should be warm.

In a small bowl, dissolve the yeast in 1/4 cup of warm water with 2 teaspoons of sugar. When it begins to foam, add the warm oil, vanilla extract, egg and confectioners sugar and beat for 1 minute or 2. Gradually add 1 cup of flour while mixing with a spatula.

Spread the remaining flour over a work surface and turn out the mixture over it. Knead gathering enough flour to form a very soft dough. Divide into 12 equal parts, cover with a kitchen towel, and let rest for 5 minutes.

Roll each piece of dough into an 8-inch rope, then fasten the two ends to form a ring. Place the rings on a floured board, cover with a kitchen towel, and let rise in a warm place for 1 hour, or until rings are doubled in bulk.

Heat the oil in a small frying pan to 375 °F on deep-frying thermometer and fry one ring at a time until golden on both sides, turning only once. Place on paper towel to drain, then roll in granulated sugar. Serve hot or at room temperature.

Yields 12.

NOTE: When stoves with ovens were a rarity in private homes, most of the baked goods were done at a public oven, and many of the smaller desserts were fried at home. I have tried *dictinobis* baked in a 375 °F oven for 20 minutes, and although the texture and even the flavor are less desirable, they have the advantage of containing less fat.

DOLCE DI MIELE
HONEY CAKE (P)

In Italy we call this cake *dolce*, sweet, instead of *torta*, cake, because the word torta presumes something roundly shaped and somewhat fancy. Honey cake can be baked in a round, square, or any other shape of pan, and it never looks very elegant. Conversely, in spite of its appearance, it is a favorite among food connoisseurs.

1/2 cup olive oil
1/2 teaspoon salt
1/4 cup sugar
4 eggs
1 cup honey
1/2 cup espresso coffee
3 tablespoons brandy
3 cups unbleached flour
2 teaspoons baking powder
1 teaspoon baking soda
1 teaspoon cinnamon
1/4 teaspoon black pepper
1/4 teaspoon ground cloves
1 teaspoon grated orange rind
1/2 cup walnut meats, coarsely chopped
1/2 cup dark seedless raisins
1/2 cup diced dates
1/4 cup diced candied orange peel
1/4 cup pinoli *(Italian pine nuts)*
10 or 12 healthy walnut or pecan halves

Cream together oil, salt, and sugar. Add the eggs, one at the time, beating constantly. Mix honey, coffee and brandy in a 2-cup measuring cup with a spout, and sift together flour, baking powder, baking soda, cinnamon, pepper, and cloves on a piece of wax paper.

Alternatively add honey and flour mixtures to the bowl. Stir in orange zest, chopped walnut meats, raisins, dates, candied orange peel, and pine nuts.

Pour into a greased loose-bottom tube cake pan. Top with the walnut or pecan halves, and bake in 375 °F oven for 45 minutes to 1 hour, or until a skewer inserted into the highest part of the cake comes out dry.

Remove to a cooling rack for 15 minutes, then invert the whole pan standing on its feet over a piece of aluminum foil; let cool thoroughly before unmolding and placing up side up on a cake dish.

Serves 12-20.

DOLCE TOSCANO DI AZZIME

TUSCAN MATZA CAKE (P)

2 regular matzot
Water
1/2 cup sugar
1 tablespoon cinnamon
1 teaspoon grated lemon rind
4 eggs, separated
Vanilla-flavored sugar (page 234)

Soak matzot in water until soft. Place the sugar with 1 tablespoon water and the cinnamon in a small pan and boil until sugar is dissolved.

Drain the matza, squeeze the water out with your hands, and place into a bowl. Add the egg yolks, the sugar/cinnamon syrup, and the lemon zest and mix well.

Beat the egg whites until stiff and dry, and fold in into the matza batter. Spoon into a greased 8-inch springform baking pan and bake in preheated 300 °F oven 45 minute or until a skewer inserted at center comes out clean.

Unmold upside down and let cool to room temperature before sprinkling it with confectioners sugar.

Serves 6-8.

DOLCETTI DI MANDORLE E DATTERI

ALMOND DATE MUNCHIES (P)

8 ounces unblanched almonds
8 ounces pitted dates
1 cup sugar
Grated rind of 1 lemon
3 egg whites
Confectioners sugar

In a blender or processor, chop the almonds very fine. Chop the dates on a board with a mezzaluna or a knife and place into a bowl. Add sugar, almonds, lemon zest, and unbeaten egg whites. Mix well to combine. Pour into a greased 8x8-inch square pan and bake in preheated 350 °F oven for 45 minutes. Remove from oven and allow to cool.

Cut into 16 squares; then cut each square into two pieces and roll each piece in confectioners sugar.

Yields 32

F

ELISIR D'AMORE
ELIXIR OF LOVE (P)

Our ancestors must have been health conscious at least as much as we are now. There is hardly any ancient recipe that is not geared to restore or improve one's health. Elixir—according to the American Heritage Dictionary of the English Language—is "any medicinal potion thought to have generalized curative or restorative powers." Donizetti built around it a funny opera, "*L'Elisir d'Amore*," in which an elixir is supposed to give a man the power of having women fall in love with him! The truth of the matter is that any liquor called "elixir" will probably have no powerful effect, other than being very agreeable to the palate (and getting you high if you drink too much of it!). When we were young we made this liqueur in many flavors, but our "love" fell on the one *al mandarino,* or tangerine-flavored elixir. My *elisir* is called *d'amore* as a spoof on the well-loved *opera buffa*, and, as it were, because it was our favorite.

In Italy these elixirs are made using pure alcohol, diluted with an equal amount of water. In America pure alcohol is not available and I have made my elixirs successfully using *acquavite** or grappa, a brandy distilled from the residue of grapevines, which is only 40-50% alcohol, and omitting water.

1 large tangerine
The peel of 4 tangerines, dried and crumbed
1 quart acquavite or grappa*
2 cups sugar
2 teaspoons vanilla extract

Chop the tangerine fine in a food processor or with a knife. Place with the dried peels in a large glass jar, add 2 cups of *acquavite* or grappa and let stand at room temperature, tightly closed, for two weeks. (Separate the lid from the jar using wax paper.) During this period shake the jar vigorously at least twice a day, changing the wax paper every few days.

Filter the tangerine mixture through a double, damp cheesecloth, then squeeze to get out as much liquid as possible. Dissolve the sugar with the remaining 2 cups of *acquavite* or grappa by slowly heating and stirring it for 2 minutes. Pour the two liquids into a glass bottle or jar. Add the vanilla extract, shake, and your elixir is ready.

Yields about 4 cups.

*The Italian *acquavite* (Latin, *aqua vitae* or French *eau de vie)* is not the Scandinavian aquavit. The latter originates from potatoes or grain while the former from wine or grape vines. Also, the latter is flavored with carraway seeds and the former is not.

ELISIR D'ARANCE
ORANGE ELIXIR (P)

Whereas *Elisir d'Amore* and *Elisir di Latte* are primarily served as after dinner liquors, *Elisir d'Arance* is also used to enhance the flavor of a variety of desserts, such as *Arance Liquorate* and *Zuccotto.*

2 small oranges or 1 large one
4 cups acquavite
2 cups sugar
2 teaspoons vanilla extract

Chop the oranges fine in a food processor. Transfer to a large glass jar, add 2 cups of acquavite and leave at room temperature, tightly closed for 2 weeks. During this period shake the jar vigorously at least twice a day.

Filter the orange mixture through a damp, double cheesecloth then squeeze to extract as much liquid as possible. Dissolve the sugar with the remaining two cups of acquavite by slowly heating and stirring it for 2 minutes. Pour the two liquids into a glass bottle or jar. Add the vanilla extract, shake, and store in your liquor cabinet.

Yields about 4 cups.

ELISIR DI LATTE
MILK ELIXIR (D)

We used to make elixir with many different fruit flavors (see the preceding recipes), but recently my sister-in-law gave me this recipe for an elixir made with milk, which is also delightful.

1 whole lemon
2 cups milk
2 1/2 cups sugar
4 cups acquavite or grappa
1 teaspoon vanilla extract
1 teaspoon almond extract

Chop the lemon fine in a processor or with a knife. Slowly heat the milk with sugar, stirring, until the sugar is dissolved, but avoid boiling the milk. Let cool to room temperature, stirring from time to time, then place in a tightly closed glass jar with lemon, acquavite, and the extracts. Leave at room temperature for 2 weeks, during which period shake the jar vigorously twice daily.

Filter through a fine sieve or coffee filter and transfer to a bottle.

Yields about 6 cups.

T

FILI D'ORO
GOLDEN THREADS (P)

This is an ancient recipe that was brought to Livorno by the Sefardim centuries ago. The golden threads are not a dessert by themselves, but are used as a garnish for the Mount Sinai made on Shavuot.

5 cups sugar
1 cup water
6 egg yolks, strained

Place the sugar and water in a saucepan over medium heat. When the solution reaches full boil, start stirring with a wooden spoon. After 3 minutes begin to test for the right cooking point of the syrup, which comes when a drop held between thumb and forefinger, in an opening and closing motion, forms a thread at the fourth opening.

Make a conic pastry bag with a sheet of white paper or a piece of plastic wrap and cut a tiny opening at the tip of the cone. Place some of the filtered egg yolk inside the bag and let it drop in a steady thread into the syrup, moving around to make separate twirls that will float at the surface of the syrup. With a slotted spoon, hold the twirls down inside the syrup and let cook for 1 minute. Remove to a large, flat strainer. Repeat until you have used up all the egg yolks. Use as directed.

FONDUTA AL CIOCCOLATO
CHOCOLATE FONDUE (D)

Fondua, in Piedmontese dialect, or fondue, as it was called in America during the rage for this dish in the late Fifties and early Sixties, is typically made with Fontina cheese as main ingredient, it is eaten by dipping chunks of bread in it, and it is served as a hors d'oeuvre, or as part of a brunch. *Fonduta al choccolato,* however, is obviously a dessert, and a fun one indeed, since it is of easy preparation and each table companion can choose what to dip in it.

18 healthy, ripe strawberries
6 bananas, peeled and sliced into 4 or 5 pieces each
6 kiwis, peeled and cut into four pieces each
24 clementine sections
24 morsels of cake
1 pound fine milk chocolate chips
1/2 cup heavy cream
1/3 cup milk

Divide the fruits and cake into 6 dishes and distribute among your guests along with 6 long fondue forks.

Place chocolate chips with cream and milk in a heavy-bottomed saucepan over low heat and stir constantly until chips are all melted. Transfer to a fondue pot for the fun of it, but avoid lighting the little light underneath it to prevent scorching of the melted chocolate.

Serve immediately, with guests dipping their fare in the hot chocolate.

Serves 6.

FRAPPE
FRIED PASTA DIAMONDS (P)

3 eggs
2 cups unbleached flour
1/2 teaspoon salt
1 1/2 cups olive or other vegetable oil for frying
Vanilla-flavored sugar (page 234)

Make a dough using the first three ingredients, then roll it down as thin as possible.

With a pizza cutter or a sharp knife, cut the pasta diagonally into many diamonds measuring approximately 7 x 4 inches. Inside each diamond, make 3 cuts widthwise.

Heat 1 cup of oil in a small, deep saucepan. Take one tip of a diamond, pass it through the slashes down-and-up-and-down, then pinch it closed to the other tip. Drop into the hot oil and fry until lightly golden. Drain over paper towel. Repeat with the remaining diamonds, frying one at the time, and adding new oil as it becomes necessary.

Arrange in layers on a serving plate, sifting abundant vanilla-flavored confectioners sugar over each layer.

Serves 12.

FRITTELLE DI CHANUKA
CHANUKAH FRITTERS (P)

This ancient recipe was a specialty of my father's oldest sister, Aunt Argia. During the eight days of Chanukah, Aunt Argia would get up at the crack of dawn to make *frittelle* for the extended family. Punctually, at meal time, she would show up at our door with a large plate of fragrant hot *frittelle*. This is the original recipe which I slightly modified to make it simpler.

3 cups unbleached flour
2 envelope active dry yeast
1 teaspoon salt
2 teaspoons anise seeds
1 cup dark seedless raisins
1 cup warm water
Olive oil
1 1/2 cups honey

Combine 2 1/2 cups flour with the yeast, salt, anise seeds and raisins in a mixing bowl. Gradually add 1 cup warm water and 2 tablespoons olive oil, mixing until a consistent dough is formed. Turn out onto a floured surface and knead for 5 minutes or until dough is smooth and elastic.

Shape into a ball, place on a floured cutting board and cover with a clean kitchen towel. Let rise in a warm place for 1 hour or until it has more than doubled in bulk.

With the palms of your hands flatten down to about 1/2-inch thickness. With the sharp, oiled blade of a long knife, cut into 36 diamonds. Let rest, uncovered, 15 or 20 minutes.

Heat enough oil in a saucepan to stand 1 1/2 inches deep. The oil is at the right temperature when a small piece of dough dropped into it comes sizzling to the surface right away. Fry a few diamonds at a time, until they are golden on both sides, turning each once. Transfer to a paper towel to drain.

Heat the honey in a saucepan and let it boil for just 3 minutes. Arrange the *frittelle* on a serving plate and pour the hot honey over them. Serve immediately.

Yields 3 dozen.

FRITTELLE DI RISO

RICE FRITTERS (P)

1/2 cup Italian or short-grain rice
1 cup water
1/4 teaspoon salt
1/2 cup dark seedless raisins
Grated rind of 1/2 lemon
2 tablespoons sugar
2 egg yolks
2 tablespoons unbleached flour
Olive oil for frying
Vanilla-flavored sugar (page 234)

Place the rice in a saucepan with cold water and salt and bring to a boil. Lower the heat to minimum, cover the pan and cook, without stirring, for 15 minutes or until very soft and dry. Remove from heat and let cool for a while, stirring occasionally. Add raisins, lemon zest, sugar, egg yolks, and flour and mix well.

Heat enough oil to stand 1/2 inch deep in a pan, add the rice mixture by the tablespoonful and gently fry until golden on all sides. Drain on paper towel. Transfer to a serving dish and sprinkle abundantly with vanilla-flavored confectioners sugar.

Yields approximately 12.

G

GELATO SI!
GELATO DI CIOCCOLATA
GELATO ALLA NOCE
GRANITA DI CAFFE
CON PANNA
GELATINA
GRANDMA'S MANDEL BROT
GELATINA DI ARANCIA
GESHMERTA MATZA
GELATO ALLA CREMA

GELATINA DI ARANCE
ORANGE JELLY (P)

I make this jelly at the time I make *Arancini* of page 33 and *Marmellata di Arance* of page 145, so that nothing goes to waste.

1 cup liquid from the orange jam of page 145.
1/2 cup sugar
1/2 cup cool orange juice
1 envelope unflavored gelatine

Place liquid from the marmalade and sugar in a small saucepan and bring to a boil. Reduce heat and simmer, uncovered, for 10 minutes. Sprinkle the gelatine over the cool orange juice in a bowl. After 1 minute, pour the hot syrup over it and stir until the gelatine is all dissolved. Wait until cool before storing in an air-tight glass jar in the refrigerator.

Yields approximately 1 1/2 cups.

GELATINA DI MELE COTOGNE
QUINCE APPLE JELLY (P)

The liquid reserved from Cotognata *(page 81)*
Sugar

Measure the liquid and place into a saucepan. For every cup of liquid, add 3/4 cup sugar. Bring to a boil.

When the liquid begins to coat the wooden spoon and has acquired an intense red color, remove from heat and place in an air-tight glass jar where it remains fresh for months.

Yields approximately 1 pint.

GELATINA DI PESCHE

PEACH JELLY (P)

The peach liquid reserved from Confettura di Pesche *(page 80)*
Apple juice or water
1 1/2 cups sugar
2 envelopes unflavored gelatine

Add enough apple juice or water to the peach liquid to measure 3 cups. Place 1 cup of liquid in a bowl and 2 cups of it and the sugar in a small saucepan. Bring to a boil, reduce the heat and simmer, uncovered, for 10 minutes. Sprinkle the gelatine over the liquid in the bowl and wait for 1 minute; then pour the hot syrup over it and stir until the gelatine is all dissolved. Wait until cool before storing in an air tight glass jar in the refrigerator.

Yields approximately 3 cups.

GELATO ALLA CREMA

VANILLA ICE CREAM (D)

This homemade gelato, a slice of cake *(Torta di Ines)*, and a small glass of sweet vermouth were all the refreshments served on the day of my Bat Mitzvah, Shavuot 1938. Yet I didn't feel I was short-changed as a girl might feel today. The ceremony was splendid, I felt I was at the center of the universe, and the simple refreshments my parents could afford seemed very luxurious to me.

The only ice cream flavors available in my village as I was growing up were vanilla and chocolate. I will give both recipes and also one for a walnut-flavored ice cream. Using these recipes and appropriate substitutions you can make other flavors that you may desire.

1 pint heavy cream
1 1/2 cups milk
1 vanilla bean, cut into 1-inch pieces

Heat cream and milk in a sauce pan with vanilla bean, then strain and set aside to cool a little.

Beat the egg yolks with sugar until frothy and lemon colored. Gradually add the warm mixture to the beaten egg yolks and keep on beating until the liquid is homogeneous. Return to the saucepan and to a moderate heat, stirring constantly with a wooden spoon until the cream begins to "smoke" and lightly coats the spoon. Strain and place in refrigerator for several hours or overnight.

Freeze in an ice cream freezer, following manufacturer directions. Transfer to a plastic container and store in the freezer, tightly covered, until ready to use.

Yields approximately 1 quart.

4 egg yolks
1 cup sugar

GELATO ALLA NOCE
WALNUT ICE CREAM (D)

Bring the milk to a gentle boil with the walnuts, honey and orange zest. Cook, stirring, for 15 - 20 minutes. Remove from heat, and let stand at room temperature until quite cool. Strain through a damp double cheese cloth, then squeeze with your hands to get as much liquid out as possible.

Beat the egg yolks with sugar until frothy and lemon colored. Add the walnut liquid, and pour into a saucepan over a moderate heat, stirring constantly with a wooden spoon, until the cream begins to "smoke" and lightly coats the spoon. Remove from heat. When cool add the whipped cream and mix to combine. Freeze in an ice cream freezer following manufacturer's directions. Transfer to a tightly covered plastic container and store in the freezer until ready to use. In order for the delicate flavor of the walnuts to fully come out, let the ice cream stand at room temperature 30 minutes before serving.

Yields approximately 1 quart.

2 cups milk
2 cups walnut meats, finely chopped
2 tablespoons honey
1/2 teaspoon grated orange peel
4 egg yolks
1/2 cup sugar
1 cup heavy cream, whipped to soft peaks

GELATO DI CIOCCOLATA
CHOCOLATE ICE CREAM (D)

1 cup heavy cream
1 1/2 cups milk
1/2 vanilla bean, cut into small pieces
3 egg yolks
8 ounces semi-sweet baking chocolate, coarsely cut up
1 tablespoon butter
1/2 cup milk chocolate chips

Heat cream and milk in a saucepan with vanilla bean, then strain and set aside to cool a little.

Beat the egg yolks with sugar until frothy and lemon colored. Gradually add the warm mixture to the beaten egg yolks and keep on beating until the liquid is homogeneous. Return to the saucepan and to a moderate heat, stirring constantly with a wooden spoon, until the cream begins to "smoke" and lightly coats the spoon. Strain and set aside.

Melt the semi-sweet chocolate with butter in a heavy-bottomed saucepan over moderate heat, stirring constantly. Add to the cream and beat to mix. Add the chocolate chips, mix, and freeze in an ice cream freezer according to manufacturer directions. Transfer to a plastic container and store in the freezer, tightly covered, until ready to use.

Yields approximately 1 quart.

GESHMEERTA MATZOS
BESMEARED MATZOT (D)

This recipe has been contributed to my collection by our good friend David Levine, the well-known painter and caricaturist, who wished thus to honor his mother, Lena Levine. Lena, like many women during World War II, was engaged in helping with the war effort. But unlike most other women, she was aware that the Russian soldiers, our Allies, also needed support. She was not rich, but she organized, among friends and neighbours, the Russian Soldier Relief by making and selling this special cake.

The following is the recipe as David passed it along to me. But in thanking you, David, I want to say that the honor is really mine, to be able to enrich my collection with the recipe of a woman endowed with such sensitivity and foresight as your mother Lena!

1/4 cup flour
4 eggs, separated
3/4 cup superfine sugar
2 1/2 pounds cottage cheese
1 pint cream
1 tablespoon lemon juice
24 plain matzos
1 cup milk
Cinnamon
Butter

Beat together flour, egg yolks, sugar, and cottage cheese. Add cream and lemon juice and mix well.

Beat the egg whites until almost stiff and fold into the mixture.

Moisten each matzo with milk on one side only. Spread the mixture on the moistened side of the matzos almost to the edge. Sprinkle with cinnamon.

Make 4 layers of 6 matzos each on a large buttered cookie sheet and bake in 350 °F oven for 15 to 20 minutes. Cut into squares.

Makes 24 squares.

GINETTI DI SUCCOT
SUKKOT COOKIES (P)

Ginetti is an ancient recipe. Like most old sweets, their appearance leaves much to be desired. Nevertheless, their taste and texture is truly fine, and for the sake of authenticity the recipe is given in its original form.

1 cup sugar
1/3 cup olive oil
1/4 teaspoon salt
2 eggs
1 cup ground blanched almonds
2 teaspoons anise seeds

Cream together sugar, oil, and salt. Add one egg at a time, beating after each addition. Add the ground almonds, anise seeds, cinnamon, orange or lemon zest, vanilla and almond extracts. Add enough flour to form a rather stiff dough. Turn out on a floured working surface, knead for 1 minute, then roll into a rope 1 inch wide. With a sharp knife, cut diagonally into 2-inch pieces.

1 teaspoon cinnamon
1 teaspoon freshly grated orange or lemon rind
1/2 teaspoon almond extract
2 cups unbleached flour

Place on a well floured sheet and bake in preheated 350 °F oven for 15 minutes. Remove from oven and transfer to a wire rack to cool.

Store in tin boxes, at room temperature, where *ginetti* keep fresh at least 8 days, the duration of sukkot.

Yields about 4 dozen.

GRANDMA RAIZEL MANDELBROT (P)

My mother-in-Law came to this country as a teenager from Minsk, the capital of Byelorussia, at the beginning of the century. Her cooking was a typical Ashkenazic fare, much of which I did not appreciate. However, besides being a warm and loving human being, Grandma was a great baker. We used to go to her house for at least one meal of each of the holidays and for all my snobbery, I did enjoy all her variations of latkes and some of her other foods. In hindsight, I wish I had recorded all of her festive repertoire. I didn't and I regret it. Luckly, though, I obtained from her recipes for some of her delightful desserts.

1/3 cup pareve margarine
1 1/4 cups sugar
1/2 teaspoon salt
4 eggs
1 1/2 teaspoons almond extract
1/4 cup vodka
1 1/2 cups whole unblanched almonds
2 teaspoons baking

Cream together margarine, sugar and salt. Add eggs, one at a time, beating after each addition. Add almond extract, vodka and almonds.

Sift together baking powder and 3 cups flour and add to the bowl 1/3 at a time while mixing. Add enough of the remaining flour to form a rather soft but manageable dough.

Turn over onto a floured work surface and divide into 4 parts. Roll each part to form 4 15-inch-long sticks.

Place on a large oiled and floured baking sheet. Bake on top rack of a 350 °F oven for 30 to 40 minutes, or until golden.

Remove from oven, and as soon as can be handled, cut diagonally to make approximately 70 2/3-inch-thick slices. Arrange on an ungreased baking sheet standing on a cut side, and bake in 450 °F oven for 10-15 minutes. Cool thoroughly before storing in tin cans.

Yields 70 or more.

powder
4 cups unbleached flour

GRANITA DI CAFFE' CON PANNA

COFFEE ICE WITH WHIPPED CREAM (D)

Sweeten the coffee with sugar while still hot. Pour into 2 plastic ice-cube containers and place the containers in the freezer for several hours or overnight.

When about ready to serve, whip the cream until soft peaks form. Add vanilla-flavored sugar and beat a few seconds longer, but be careful not to overbeat and end up with butter.

Crush the coffee cubes in an electric crusher and distribute evenly among the chilled glasses. Add 1 tablespoon liqueur to each glass and top with whipped cream. Serve immediately.

Serves 6.

4 cups freshly-made espresso
1/4 cup sugar
6 tablespoons brandy or anisette
1 pint heavy cream
1/3 cup vanilla-flavored sugar (page 234)
6 fluted glasses, chilled

NOTE: If you don't have an electric ice crusher, place a few cubes at a time inside a clean cloth and pound with a hammer, the good old way. Don't attempt to do the crushing in a food processor or the granita (hail-like pieces of ice) will become snow and the texture will be lost.

H

HAMANTASCHEN
FILLED COOKIES (P)

Hamantaschen (Haman's pockets) is a typical Ashkenazic Purim dessert, much as *Orecchi di Aman* (Haman's Ears) is the Purim dessert par excellence for the Italian Jews. It is called Haman's pockets because the pastry is filled as in a pocket, but the shape of these cookies resembles more the tricornered hat presumably worn by the wicked Haman.

Hamantaschen can be prepared with a number of different fillings, and one's imagination is the only limit. The following recipe calls for the popular poppy-seed filling.

POPPY SEED FILLING:

1 cup poppy seeds, ground or whole
1/2 cup water
1/4 cup seedless dark raisins
1/2 cup honey
2 tablespoons sugar
1 teaspoon grated lemon rind
2 teaspoons finely chopped orange rind
2 cinnamon Graham crakers, crumbed

PASTRY:

2 eggs
2 egg yolks
1/2 cup sugar
1/2 teaspoon salt
1 teaspoon freshly grated lemon rind
1/4 cup olive oil
1 teaspoon vanilla extract
2 tablespoons vodka or brandy
1 teaspoon baking powder
2 1/2 cups unbleached flour

Place the poppy seeds (preferably ground, if you own a coffee grinder), water, raisins, honey, sugar, lemon zest and orange rind in a small saucepan and bring to a gentle boil. Simmer for 10 minutes, stirring frequently. Remove from heat, add the crumbed crackers, stir, then chill until ready to use. It is desirable, but not imperative, to prepare the filling a few days in advance.

In a small bowl beat the eggs and egg yolks with sugar, salt, lemon zest, oil, vanilla extract and vodka. Add baking powder and gradually add enough flour to form a rather soft dough. Turn out onto a floured surface and knead a couple of minutes. Roll very thin, taking care not to tear it.

With a round pastry cutter or a wine glass 3 inches in diameter, cut discs. Place a tablespoon of filling at center of each disc, then pull up the edge on three sides and pinch these sides together to resemble tricornered hats.

Place the hamantaschen on a lightly oiled and floured baking sheet about 1 inch apart, and bake in preheated 350 °F oven for 12-15 minutes. Remove to cooling rack and serve at room temperature.

Yields 24 to 36.

I

IMPADE
ALMOND-FILLED HALF MOONS (P)

Dissolve 1/2 cup sugar with 2 tablespoons water in a saucepan over moderately high heat for 2 minutes, stirring frequently. Off the heat add almonds, pinoli, raisins, 2 egg yolks and rum and mix to combine.

Mix together 2 1/2 cups flour, 1/2 teaspoon salt, all the margarine, 2 egg yolks and two eggs. Turn over onto a floured surface and knead, adding flour as needed to make a consistent dough. Roll thin and cut into disks with a 3-inch round cookie cutter or a wine glass. Place a tablespoon of filling off the center of each disk, moisten the rim with some of the finishing egg white and close. Poke a few holes with prong of a fork.

Arrange on ungreased cookie sheet, lightly brush the tops with egg white, and sprinkle abundantly with sugar. Bake in 350 °F oven for 25 minutes or until tops are golden brown. Cool on rack.

Yields approximately 2 dozen.

FILLING:

1/2 cup sugar
2 tablespoons water
2 1/2 cups (10 ounces) ground blanched almonds
1/2 cup pinoli *(Italian pine nuts)*
1/4 cup malaga raisins
2 egg yolks
2 tablespoons rum

PASTRY:

3 cups flour
1/2 teaspoon salt
1/2 pound plus 2 tablespoons parve margarine, softened
2 egg yolks
2 eggs, slightly beaten

TO FINISH:

2 egg whites slightly beaten with a pinch of salt
1/2 cup sugar

INSALATA DI FRUTTA
FRUIT SALAD (P)

For the Italian version of this salad see *Macedonia di Frutta*.

INSALATA DI FRUTTA SECCA
DRIED FRUIT SALAD (P)

I should call this dessert "life saver" because when I have unexpected guests and no time to make a dessert, this nutty/fruity mixture will fill the bill deliciously. A mixture of your favorite dried fruit and nuts should be at hand at all times, not only as a healthy munch, but also because when needed, with the addition of your favorite liqueur, it can be easily converted into a dessert for your guests. Below is only an indication of the type of dried fruit you can put together.

1 cup hazelnuts
1 cup whole almonds
1/2 cup pinoli *(Italian pine nuts)*
1/2 cup pecan meat
1/2 cup walnut meat
1/2 cup dried cranberries
1 cup seedless raisins
1/2 cup dried cherries
1/2 cup chopped dried figs
1/2 cup pitted dates
1 cup chocolate liqueur (page 137)

Mix together all the nuts and dried fruits, and keep in a cookie jar for anyone in the family to enjoy as a snack. When you want to use this mixture as a dessert for your guests, chop in a food processor not too fine, add the liqueur at the last possible moment, toss, and serve.

Serves 12.

INSALATA DI RISO DOLCE
SWEET RICE SALAD (D)

1 1/2 cups rice
2 cups water
1/2 teaspoon salt
1 cup milk, hot
2 tablespoons sugar
grated rind of 1 lemon
1/2 cup white seedless raisins
1/2 cup dried cherries
2 kiwi fruits, peeled and diced
Cinnamon sugar
1/4 cup Elisir d'Amore *or* Elisir d'Arance

Place the rice in a saucepan with water and salt and bring to a gentle boil. Cook, covered, for 10 minutes without stirring. Add milk, sugar, and lemon zest and cook uncovered, stirring frequently, another 5 to 10 minutes, or until the rice is done and dry. Remove from heat and spread over a large plate to cool.

Soak raisins and cherries in hot water for 5 minutes, then drain and add to the rice. Add the kiwi and toss to combine. Refrigerate until ready to serve. Sprinkle with cinnamon sugar and liquor.

Serves 6.

LA PATTONA
CHESTNUT POLENTA (D)

Pattona is not a very elegant dessert and you wouldn't want to make it for company. But it was one of the fun foods of my childhood and I like to share it with my readership. Children will certainly appreciate it.

3 cups water
1 teaspoon salt
3 cups chestnut flour
1 pint ricotta
Cinnamon sugar, optional

Bring 3 cups of water with 1 teaspoon salt to a boil in a saucepan. Sift chestnut flour and add to the boiling water all at once, stirring vigorously with a wooden spoon. As soon as the mass gathers into a single lump, remove from heat and pour out onto a board or a dish. Cover with a clean kitchen towel and let rest for a couple of minutes, then slice and serve topped with ricotta. Serve as is or sprinkled with cinnamon sugar.

Serves 6 or more.

LATKES
FRIED SMALL PANCAKES (D OR P)

The word "latkes" in Yiddish is used to designate any chopped vegetable or fruit held together with eggs and some starch fried in oil. I will describe only one dessert latke as an example and you can use your imagination to make variations on this theme.

3 large apples, peeled, cored and chopped
1 cup walnut meat, chopped
1 tablespoon potato starch
1 tablespoon rum
3 eggs, slightly beaten
Oil for frying
Vanilla-flavored sugar (page 234)

Place the apples and nuts in a bowl. Dissolve the starch in the rum and add to the bowl. Add eggs and mix well.

Fry by the tablespoonful in hot oil until golden on both sides, turning only once. Drain on paper. Arrange on a serving plate and sprinkle abundantly confectioner's sugar.

Serves 6.

LATTE ALLA PORTOGHESE
CARAMEL CUSTARD (D)

This dessert, known all over the world as flan, was undoubtedly brought to Italy by the Sephardim who had fled the Iberian peninsula during the later stage of the Spanish Inquisition when they were also expelled from Portugal.

2 cups sugar
1 egg
7 egg yolks
1 quart milk
2 1/2x2-inches strips of lemon peel
1 teaspoon grated lemon rind
1 teaspoon vanilla extract

Cook 1 cup of sugar with a few drops of water until melted and dark brown. Pour into 1 1/2-quart souffle dish or into 10 individual ramekins. Tilt the container or the ramekins to completely coat the bottom and part of the sides.

Beat the egg and egg yolks with 1 cup of sugar until fluffy and lemon colored.

Bring the milk with lemon peels to a boil in a heavy-bottomed saucepan, lower the heat, and cook 10 minutes, stirring often to make sure that it does not stick to the bottom and scorch. Strain and add the lemon zest and the vanilla extract. Cool for a while, then gradually add to the beaten egg-sugar mixture, mixing well.

Pour into the souffle dish or the individual ramekins and place in a shallow pan with 1/2 inch of warm water.

Bake in 350 °F oven for 30 to 45 minutes, or until tops are browned and a skewer inserted at center of custard comes out clean. Let cool at room temperature, then refrigerate, loosely covered with wax paper, until ready to serve.

With a thin blade separate custard from container wall, then invert over a serving dish or individual dessert dishes.

Serves 8 to 10.

LATTE DI MANDORLE

ALMOND MILK (P)

This "milk" was used by us in place of milk to convert a dessert from dairy to pareve. However, many Sephardim use it mainly as a drink to break the fast of Yom Kippur. Try it as an addition to your breakfast cereal for a new taste experience.

10 ounces blanched almonds
2 cups boiled water, warm

In the bowl of a food processor fitted with the metal blade, place the almonds and process for a full minute.

Gradually add the warm water and keep on processing for another 20 seconds. Transfer to an airtight jar and store in the refrigerator.

Yields approximately 2 1/2 cups.

LEAH'S TAMARIM BISCUITS

DATE COOKIES FROM KURDISTAN (P)

Leah and my daughter Gia spent their freshman year in Israel studying and working. In the Moshav where she worked, Leah learned from the Kurdish mother to make these cookies and made me promise that if I ever wrote a dessert book, I would include them in it. Here they are.

1 1/2 cups sugar
3/4 cup (6 ounces) pareve margarine
2 eggs
1 teaspoon vanilla extract
5 cups unbleached flour
3 teaspoons baking

Cream together sugar and margarine. Add the eggs one at the time, beating after each addition. Add vanilla extract and mix. Sift together 1 cup of flour with the baking powder and add to the mixture. Add enough of the remaining flour to form a rather soft dough.

Turn over onto a floured work surface and add flour as needed for the dough to be manageable, then divide into four equal parts. Over a pastry cloth roll each piece

powder
1 1/2 cups date butter (see recipe below)
Hulled sesame seeds

of dough down to form a 6x9-inch rectangle. Spread one fourth of the date butter over each rectangle, leaving 1/2-inch margin all around. With the help of the pastry cloth, roll lengthwise as for a jelly roll and tuck under.

Cut each roll into 1/2-inch slices and arrange on a greased and floured baking sheet. Sprinkle with sesame seeds and bake in preheat 350 °F oven for 15 minutes or until lightly brown.

Yields about 5 dozen.

BURRO DI DATTERI
DATE BUTTER (P)

If you don't find the date butter in your specialty store, you can easily make it yourself.

10 ounces pitted dates
1/2 seedless orange (including peel), diced
1 teaspoon cinnamon
2 cups water

Place all the ingredients into a food processor or blender and process until all is liquefied. Pour into a saucepan and bring to a rapid boil. Lower the heat and simmer uncovered, stirring occasionally, until reduced to 1 1/2 cups. Remove to a glass container and refrigerate until ready to use.

Yields 1 1/2 cups.

LIQUORE AL CIOCCOLATO
CHOCOLATE LIQUOR (D)

2 cups milk
1 1/2 cups sugar
5 ounces unsweetened baking chocolate
1 cup cream
1 teaspoon vanilla extract
2 cups acquavite

In a small saucepan bring 2 cups of milk with the sugar to a boil, then lower the heat and let simmer for 12 minutes. Remove from heat. In another saucepan, over moderate heat, dissolve the chocolate with one cup of cream. Add the warm milk mixture, bring to a gentle boil and whisk constantly for another 5 minutes.

Remove from heat and when thoroughly cool add vanilla extract and acquavite. Transfer to a glass bottle and shake well before using.

Yields approximately 1 quart.

M

MACEDONIA DI FRUTTA
MIXED FRUIT DESSERT (P)

This is a typical Italian dessert, served in quality restaurants and at important dinners, not to be confused with an ordinary fruit salad.

1/2 cup cantaloupe balls
1 large pear, peeled, cored and diced
2 bananas, peeled and diced
1 large peach, pitted and diced
1 nectarine, pitted and diced
1 pint fresh, ripe strawberries, sliced
1/2 cup raspberries
1/4 cup fresh, red currant
2 kiwis peeled and diced
1/4 cup pinoli *(Italian pine nuts) or 1/4 cup peeled almond slivers*
2/3 cup sugar
1/4 cup water
6 tablespoons fruit liqueur

In a serving bowl, place all the fruit and nuts and delicately toss before storing temporarily in refrigerator.

Place sugar and water in a small saucepan over high heat. Bring to a boil and cook for 5 minutes. Remove from heat and let cool at room temperature.

Add the liqueur to the sugar syrup, stir and pour over the fruit. Mix gently and serve.

Serves 6.

MACRUTE

TYPICAL LIBYAN PURIM SWEET (P)

Macrute or macrote is one of the several recipes my Florentine friend Wanda Nahum Caro, a native of Tripoli, Libya, has given me in the course of years.

1 pound coarse semolina or farina
1/4 cup unbleached flour
Olive oil
1/4 cup water
1/2 pound pitted dates, chopped
1/2 teaspoon ground cloves
1 teaspoon cinnamon
1 teaspoon ground ginger
1/4 teaspoon grated nutmeg
1 cup honey
1/2 cup water
Toasted sesame seeds

Combine and thoroughly mix the semolina with flour, 3/4 cup warm olive oil and 1/4 cup water. Roll out on a flat surface to a 1/2-inch thickness.

Place the dates, cloves, cinnamon, ginger and nutmeg in the skillet with the 2 tablespoons oil, and mix over low heat until a homogeneous paste is formed. Spread over half the rolled-out semolina and cover with the other half. Cut into 24 parts. Take one at a time and, with your oiled hands, form egg-shaped balls, making sure that the date paste is enclosed in the semolina.

Line on a lightly oiled and floured baking sheet and bake in 300 °F oven for 1/2 hour. Allow to cool at room temperature. Place the honey and 1/2 cup water in a saucepan and bring to a boil. Cook 3 minutes, then lower the temperature and simmer the macrute balls inside the syrup for 1 minute. Lift with a slotted spoon and arrange on a serving dish. Sprinkle with sesame seeds and serve.

Yields 24.

MANICOTTI DI PURIM
PURIM MANICOTTI (P)

This is one of those recipes one should watch while it is being prepared, because the actual preparation is much less complicated than its description. The aid of a manual pasta machine would be helpful, but not indispensable.

2 eggs
1/8 teaspoon salt
1 1/2 cups unbleached flour
1 cup olive oil or other vegetable oil for frying
1 1/2 cups honey

Lightly beat eggs and salt together. Gradually add 1 1/4 to 1 1/2 cups of flour and mix until a rather soft dough is formed. Turn over unto a floured surface and knead for 1 minute or so, then roll down as thin as you can. With a very sharp knife or a pizza cutter, make 24 strips, approximately 2x8 inches.

Heat the oil in a small frying pan. Holding one strip of dough at one end with your hand, plunge the other end into the hot oil 1 inch deep. At once insert the frying part of the strip between the prongs of a fork held with your other hand, and roll the fork while letting the rest of the strip slide into the oil. The strip will fry while it is rolling around the fork.

When the *manicotto* is golden, remove from oil and gently place on a paper towel. Repeat until all *manicotti* are done.

Heat half the honey in a small saucepan. As it starts to boil, drop 2 or 3 manicotti in it for a few seconds to be coated with honey, then transfer to a serving dish. Lower the heat and continue to dip the manicotti, gradually adding more honey, until all have been coated. Cool thoroughly before serving.

Yields 24.

MARITOZZI COLLA PANNA

CREAM-FILLED SWEET BUNS (D)

Maritozzi colla Panna was the breakfast with which our Grandmother Fiorina in Rome treated us when we were little children and our mother took us to visit her. On October 16, 1943, Grandmother was among the two thousand deportees to the German death camps. Today I serve it whenever I want to eulogize her gentleness and recreate in my mind the magic of those years before the inferno opened under our feet. But I also serve this nutricious and delicious alternative to cereal on special occasions, such as birthdays, or when I have guests.

1 envelope active dry yeast
1/2 cup warm water
1 small pinch of salt
1/4 cup sugar
1 3/4 cups unbleached flour
2 tablespoons olive oil
1/4 cup seedless raisins
1 heaping tablespoon candied orange peel, finely chopped
1 heaping tablespoon pinoli *(Italian pine nuts)*
1 egg beaten with a small pinch salt
1 pint heavy cream

Place the yeast in a small bowl with the warm water, salt, 1 teaspoon sugar, and 1/4 cup flour. Mix and let rest at room temperature for 20 minutes. Add sugar, oil, raisins, candied orange peel, *pinoli*, and the remaining flour and mix to form a rather soft dough. Let it rest in a warm place for 45 minutes or until doubled.

Turn out over a floured surface and divide into 8 equal parts. Give each an oval shape, and place on an ungreased non-stick baking sheet. Cover with a clean towel and let rest in a warm place for 1/2 hour, or until the little buns have doubled their volume.

Brush the tops with the beaten egg and place in preheated 450 °F oven for 7 minutes, or until tops are golden brown. Remove from oven.

Beat the cream until soft peaks form. Make a cut along the length of each bun, but do not slice completely through. Delicately open the cut sides of the buns and fill them with whipped cream.

Yields 8.

MARMELLATA DI ARANCE
ORANGE JAM (P)

Cut the oranges over a dish into small pieces. Place in a saucepan and gradually bring to a boil. Lower the heat to minimum and let simmer, covered, for 20 to 30 minutes.

Strain and reserve the juice (approximately 1 cup) for the jelly of page 113.

Weigh the cooked orange pulp and place in a saucepan with half its weight of sugar. Bring to a boil, then lower the heat and simmer, uncovered, 30 to 40 minutes. Pour into an air-tight glass jar and store in refrigerator.

Yields approximately 1 pint.

6 large oranges, peeled
Sugar

MARMELLATA DI ARANCE DI MARCELLA
MARCELLA'S ORANGE MARMALADE (P)

Keep the oranges and lemon in a pot with fresh water for a few hours, then place on the heat and bring to a boil. Lower the heat and simmer until peels become soft—approximately 30 minutes.

Drain and, as soon as can be handled, cut the oranges and the lemon in half lengthwise. Cut the lemon and some of the oranges into tiny wedges, and the rest in chunks. Chop a few chunks at a time in a processor for 10 seconds.

Weigh wedges and chopped oranges with all their juice, and place in a heavy-bottomed pot with equal weight of sugar. Bring to a boil, then simmer, uncovered, stirring occasionally with a wooden spoon. When the spoon comes out coated with a dense syrup (30 to 45 minutes), remove from heat, add the vanilla extract and stir. Store in air-tight glass jars.

Yields approximately 2 pints.

3 pounds oranges
1 lemon
Water
Sugar
1 1/2 teaspoons vanilla extract

MARMELLATA DI CASTAGNE
CHESTNUT CREAM (P)

2 pounds fresh, healthy chestnuts
1/2 teaspoon anise seeds
1/2 teaspoon salt
2 1/2 cups sugar
2 1/2 cups water
1 teaspoon vanilla extract

Remove outer dark-brown shell from chestnuts. Place in a saucepan with anise seeds, salt, and enough water to cover. Bring to a boil, then simmer, covered, until tender—20 to 30 minutes. Drain.

Peel off the inner skin and pass through a sieve. Place in a saucepan with all the sugar and 1 cup of water and bring to a gentle boil. Cook on low heat, stirring almost constantly, for approximately 30 minutes. Add a few tablespoons of water if it becomes necessary to prevent cream from becoming too thick.

Remove from heat, add vanilla extract, and stir. Pour into air-tight glass jars and store at room temperature.

Yields approximately 3 cups.

MARRONCINI
PURIM NUT COOKIES (P)

The name *marroncini* derives from the Hebrew *maror*, bitter. These cookies were given their name because the Jews in Pitigliano used the almonds of peach pits to make them, and those almonds are bitter indeed! I recall that after drying the pits in the sun, they were saved in old pillow cases throughout the entire peach season. We were aware that they contained prussic acid, which is poisonous, but we also knew that our ancestors, who had been eating *marroncini* all their lives, had enjoyed good health and many reached ripe old ages. At any rate, the so-called almond extract one buys on the American markets today *is* made from peach-pit almonds! I have seen *marroncini* made (and make them myself) with hazel nuts or sweet almonds and almond extract, and they are simply delicious.

3 cups unbleached flour
*1 1/2 cups coarsely chopped hazel nuts or almonds, toasted**
*1/2 teaspoon ammonium bicarbonate*** or 1 teaspoon baking powder*
Grated rind of 1 lemon
1 1/2 cups sugar
2 cups cold water
1 1/2 teaspoons almond extract

Combine nuts, flour, baking powder, and lemon rind and mix well. Mound on a work surface or in a large bowl and make a well in the center.

Place the sugar and 2 cups of cold water in a saucepan and bring to a boil. When the solution reaches full boil, start stirring with a wooden spoon. After 3 minutes, begin to test for the right cooking point of the syrup, which comes when a drop held between thumb and forefinger, in an opening and closing motion, forms a thread at the fourth opening.

Add almond extract, stir, and pour into the center of the well. Quickly mix in the dry ingredients and, also quickly, knead for a minute or so.

Divide the dough into 4 parts, and roll each part into a cylinder 1 1/2 inches in diameter. Cut each cylinder into 1-inch-thick disks. With your thumb, make a depression at the center of each disk. Coat with the flour mixture that has remained on the work surface or bowl.

Place in a well-floured baking sheet and bake in preheated 400 °F oven for 15 to 20 minutes. Cookies are done when the bottom is golden brown.

Yields about 50.

* To toast the nuts, place them in single layer on a baking sheet and place the sheet under the broiler for 4 to 5 minutes, shaking the sheet a couple of times. Allow to cool at least 10 minutes before chopping.

** Ammonium bicarbonate can be purchased from pharmacies. It is *not* the same as sodium bicarbonate (baking soda) available in supermarkets.

MARZAPANE
MARZIPAN (P)

1 pound blanched almonds
1 1/2 cups sugar
1/4 cup water
1 teaspoon almond extract
1 teaspoon grated lemon rind

Place half the almonds in a food processor and process for 15 seconds or until the almonds are pulverized. Repeat with the remaining almonds.

Place the sugar and water in a saucepan over medium heat. When the solution reaches full boil, start stirring with a wooden spoon. After 3 minutes begin to test for the right cooking point of the syrup,which comes when a drop held between thumb and forefinger, in an opening and closing motion, forms a thread at the fourth opening.

Add the finely chopped almonds, almond extract and lemon zest, stir and immediately remove from heat. Turn out over a lightly floured surface and knead until you have a homogeneous paste.

Use as directed.

MATZA COPERTA
MATZA OMELET (P)

It is customary for Catholics in Italy to go for a picnic on the Monday following Easter Sunday. When we were children our Catholic friends would invite us to join in the feast. We would gladly go, but would bring our own kosher foods. Our typical basket contained hard boiled eggs, a few slices of homemade cold cuts, carciofi trifolati (slivered artichokes sauteed in olive oil), and *matza coperta*.

6 regular matzot
12 eggs, slightly beaten
1/2 teaspoon salt

Soak the matzot in cold water until they are soft. Drain and squeeze the water out, but do not leave the matzot too dry. Combine with eggs, salt, raisins, nuts, and lemon zest.

1/2 cup dark, seedless raisins
1/4 cup pinoli *(Italian pine nuts)*
Freshly grated rind of 1 lemon
6 tablespoons olive oil
Cinnamon sugar

Heat 3 tablespoons of oil in a large, heavy skillet. Add the matza mixture and flatten down with a rubber spatula. Fry gently on very low heat, shaking the skillet from time to time, until a light crust is formed at the bottom. Invert onto a large dish.

Return the skillet over the low heat, add the remaining 3 tablespoons of oil and slide the omelet into it. Fry gently until a crust is formed also on the other side. The omelet is done when it is firm all the way through.

Place on a serving plate and pat dry with a paper towel. Top omelet with cinnamon sugar and serve.

Serves 8-12.

MELE FRITTE
FRIED APPLE RINGS (P)

6 large cooking apples
Cinnamon sugar
1/4 cup fruit liqueur such as Elisir d'Amore
Olive oil
1 cup unbleached flour
1 teaspoon baking powder
1/2 teaspoon salt
1/2 teaspoon freshly grated lemon rind
3/4 cup water
Vanilla-flavored sugar (page 234)

Pare the apples and cut horizontally into 1/4-inch slices. Remove the core and place in a bowl in layers, sprinkling each layer with cinnamon sugar. Add the liqueur and set aside to marinate for at least 1 hour. Drain and reserve the liquid.

Heat 1 1/2 cups of oil in a large frying pan. Mix together flour, baking powder, salt and lemon zest. Add water, the liquid from the marinate, and 2 tablespoons of oil and quickly stir to mix. Dip a few rings at a time in the batter, then fry in the hot oil until golden brown on both sides. Drain on paper towel. Sprinkle with vanilla-flavored confectioners sugar and serve.

Serves 6.

MOHNKUCHEN
POPPYSEED CAKE (D)

A dear friend in Ottawa once made this cake for us as my husband and I were visiting. I liked it very much, and although I had never heard of desserts made with poppy seeds in Italy, as a married woman in America I learned from my mother-in-law about hamantachen, strudel and cakes made with poppy seeds. Here is my friend Fran's version with my personal touch.

2 tablespoons soft butter
2 tablespoons fine bread crumbs
*6 ounces poppyseeds, crushed**
3/4 cup milk
4 tablespoons butter, melted and cooled to room tempera ture
1 teaspoon vanilla extract, optional
5 eggs, separated
1 cup sugar
1/4 teaspoon cream of tartar
6 ounces (1 1/2 cups) unblanched al-monds, ground

Grease with 2 tablespoons butter and sprinkle with bread crumbs a 10-inch springform cake pan, and set aside.

Combine crushed poppy seeds and milk in a saucepan. Gently bring to a boil and stir until the seeds have absorbed all the milk—5 to 10 minutes. Allow to cool, then add melted butter, vanilla extract, if you choose to use it, and stir.

Beat the egg whites with cream of tartar until stiff and dry. With the beaters on, gradually add 1/2 cup sugar. Set aside.

Beat the egg yolks with the remaining 1/2 cup sugar until smooth and lemon colored. Add the ground almonds and mix. Add the poppyseed mixture and mix. Gently fold in beaten egg white, and turn into the prepared cake pan.

Bake in preheated 350 °F oven for 45 minutes. Cake is done when the center is slightly firm and sides begin to come away from the pan. Cool thoroughly over cooling rack, then turn upside down on a cake dish.

Serves 12.

* Crush the poppy seeds in a blender or in a coffee grinder, if you own one, otherwise use them uncrushed.

MOHN STRUDEL
POPPYSEED YEAST STRUDEL (D)

2 envelopes dry yeast
1/2 cup orange juice at room temperature
Pinch salt
1 cup vegetable oil
1/2 cup sugar
5 eggs
2 cups milk, warm
3 cups unbleached flour
8 ounces poppyseeds, crushed (see preceding recipe)
1/4 cup honey
1/2 cup chopped walnut meats
1 teaspoon vanilla extract, optional

Dissolve the yeast in the orange juice with a pinch of salt and let rest for about 5 minutes. Cream together the oil and the sugar. Add 4 eggs, one at a time, beating after each addition.

Add 1 cup of milk and the yeast mixture. Add enough flour to make a consistent dough. Cover and set aside to rise in a warm place.

Meanwhile prepare the filling. Place the poppy seeds, the remaining cup of milk and the honey in a saucepan and gently boil, stirring occasionally, until the mixture has become thick. Remove from heat and add nuts and vanilla extract, if you choose to use it, mixing well. Let cool.

Turn the dough over a pastry sheet or tablecloth. Roll down as thin as you can, forming a rectangle. Spread the poppyseed mixture over the dough, then roll as for a jelly roll, tuck under, cover, and set aside to rise again for 1 to 2 hours.

Beat the remaining egg with a small pinch of salt and brush the top of the roll. Bake in 350 °F oven for one hour or until the top is golden brown.

Serves 12.

MONTE SINAI

MOUNT SINAI (P)

1 recipe Marzapane
4 tablespoons candied citron peel, chopped fine
1 recipe Fili d'Oro
1 small egg, slightly beaten with a pinch of salt

Take the *marzapane* and divide it into 4 uneven pieces, each larger than the next. Make a ball of each piece and flatten the 3 larger ones down to form disks. Sprinkle the largest with 1 1/2 tablespoons citron peel. Cover with the second larger disk, and sprinkle with 1 tablespoon citron peel. Cover with the third disk and sprinkle it with the remaining citron peel. Top with the smallest ball, slightly flattened at bottom.

Brush the mount with beaten egg and garnish with the *fili d'oro*. Place on a baking dish and bake in preheated 300 °F oven for 10 minutes. Serve at room temperature on the festival of Shavuot.

Serves 8.

MOSCARDINI DI PESACH

ALMOND MACAROONS (P)

1 1/2 cups ground toasted almonds
1 cup sugar
Small pinch salt
1/4 cup unsweetened cocoa
1/4 cup matza meal
Grated rind of 1 orange
1/2 teaspoon almond extract
1 egg, slightly beaten
1 egg yolk
Oil and matza meal for the baking sheet

Combine the first 9 ingredients in a small bowl and mix well. Drop the mixture with a small scoop on a baking sheet previously oiled and dusted with matza meal 1 1/2 inches apart.

Bake in preheated 350 °F oven for 12 minutes, then transfer to a cooling rack.

Yields approximately 2 1/2 dozen.

MOSCARDINI DI PESACH II

PASSOVER MOSCARDINI II (P)

Cream olive oil and sugar in a large bowl. Add the eggs, one at a time, beating after each addition. Add salt, walnuts and melted chocolate and mix well.

Chop the orange with all its peel fine and add to the bowl. Add 2 1/2 cups matza meal and stir to combine.

Oil and dust with matza meal a 10x15-inches baking sheet with raised borders. Pour the batter into it, flatten evenly with a rubber spatula and bake in 350 °F oven for 30 minutes. Remove from heat and let cool to room temperature. With a sharp knife or pizza cutter, make 6 cuts lengthwise and 9 diagonally. Cool thoroughly before transferring the diamonds to a cookie jar.

Yields approximately 4 dozen.

1/2 cup olive oil
1 cup sugar
4 eggs
Pinch of salt
1 cup chopped walnuts
8 ounces semisweet baking chocolate, melted
1 seedless orange, washed and quartered
3 cups matza meal
Oil for the baking sheet

MOSCARDINI DI PURIM

PURIM MOSCARDINI (P)

Combine all the dry ingredients in a small bowl. Add the egg and egg yolk and mix well. Shape the mixture with your hands, a teaspoonful at a time, into 3-inch oval balls. Place on an oiled and floured baking sheet 2 1/2 inches apart and flatten down with a fork.

Bake in preheated 350 °F oven for 10 minutes, then transfer to a cooling rack.

Yields about 2 1/2 dozen.

1 1/4 cups ground toasted almonds
1 1/4 cups sugar
1/4 cup unsweetened cocoa
1/4 cup unbleached flour
1/2 teaspoon ground cinnamon
1 egg, slightly beaten
1 egg yolk

MUCCHIETTI DI MANDORLE
ALMOND MOUNDS (P)

2 egg whites
dash salt
1 cup sugar
1 teaspoon grated lemon peel
1 teaspoon almond extract
1 teaspoon vanilla extract
2 cups sliced peeled almonds
2 tablespoons pareve margarine

Beat the egg whites with salt until firm and dry. Add sugar, lemon zest, almond and vanilla extracts, and finally the sliced almonds.

Grease the baking sheet with margarine and spoon small mounds of the mixture 2 inches apart. Bake in preheated 300 °F oven for 12 minutes. Transfer to cooling rack.

Yields 2 or 2 1/2 dozen.

MUSTACCHIONI
CHOCOLATE ALMOND COOKIES (P)

1 pound almonds, peel on
1 pound semisweet chocolate chips
1 cup sugar
4 eggs, slightly beaten
2 tablespoons pareve margarine

Roast the almonds under the broiler and when cool, chop not too fine and place into a bowl. Chop the chocolate chips coarsely and add to the bowl. Add the sugar and mix to combine.

Gradually add the eggs, stirring until the dry ingredients are moist. Grease a baking sheet with the margarine. Drop on it the mixture using a tablespoon held horizontally to make oval-shaped cookies. Bake in 400 °F oven for 10 to 15 minutes. Cookies should result crisp outside but soft inside.

Yields 3 dozen.

MUSTACCHIONI II

CHOCOLATE ALMOND COOKIES II (P)

10 ounces (2 1/2 cups) peeled almonds, finely chopped
1 cup sugar
1/2 cup diced candied citron peel
1/2 cup unsweetened cocoa
2 tablespoons flour
2 tablespoons rum
3 eggs, slightly beaten
Vanilla-flavored sugar (page 234)
2 tablespoons pareve margarine

Mix together all the dry ingredients. Gradually add the rum and the eggs, stirring until you have a homogeneous paste. Grease the baking sheet with margarine and drop the almond mixture over it, using a tablespoon held horizontally to make oval-shaped cookies. Bake in 350 °F oven for 12 minutes. Remove to cooling rack. When thoroughly cool, top with vanilla-flavored confectioners sugar, using a small sifter.

Yields 3 dozen.

N

NOCIATINE
WALNUT MUNCHIES (P)

Bring the honey to a boil in a saucepan and cook, stirring, for 7 minutes. Add the chopped walnuts, orange zest, cinnamon and cloves and cook another 7 minutes, stirring. Remove from heat and keep on stirring for a few more minutes.

Oil a cutting board and cover with aluminum foil. Sprinkle some water over the foil, then spoon the hot mixture forming mounds. With a wet wooden spatula flatten down. Wait until thoroughly cool before removing from board and peeling off aluminum foil.

Yields 12 to 16.

1 cup honey
1 1/2 cups chopped walnut meats
2 tablespoons grated orange peel
1 teaspoon ground cinnamon
1/4 teaspoon ground cloves
2 tablespoons oil

NOCCIOLE AL CIOCCOLATO
CHOCOLATE-COVERED HAZELNUTS (D)

Toast the hazelnuts until the peels are black. When cool enough to handle, peel them by rubbing a few at a time between the palms of your hands. A few pieces of peel will remain, but it is all right. Let cool to room temperature.

Dissolve all the chocolate and butter in a heavy bottomed pan over very low heat. Stir constantly with a rubber spatula until all chocolate is melted. Remove from heat, add vanilla and keep on stirring until cooled a little—about 2 minutes. Add 1/3 of the nuts and stir until they are all coated. Lift one by one with a fork and spread on a large piece of wax paper over a cutting board. Slightly reheat the melted chocolate and stir to cool it a little. Procede with the other two thirds of nuts in the same fashion as the first third. Place the board in the refrigerator for 12 to 15 minutes, then leave at room temperature for several hours or overnight. Remove from wax paper and store in cookie jar at room temperature.

Yields about 3 cups.

1 1/2 cups hazelnuts (filberts)
8 ounces semi-sweet baking chocolate, cut up
8 ounces milk chocolate, cut up
1 tablespoon sweet butter
2 teaspoons vanilla extract

O

ORECCHI DI AMAN
HAMAN'S EARS (P)

For the Italian Jews *orecchi di Aman* are as synonymous with the festival of Purim as *Hamantachen* are for the Ashkenazim. There are perhaps as many versions of this sweet as there are Jewish families in Italy. I regard this recipe as the finest. From this basic recipe you can create variations limited only by your own imagination.

2 eggs
2 egg yolks
1/4 cup sugar
1/2 teaspoon salt
1 teaspoon freshly ground lemon rind
2 tablespoons olive oil
1 teaspoon vanilla extract
2 tablespoons rum or brandy
2 1/2 cups unbleached flour
1 cup olive or other vegetable oil for frying
Vanilla-flavored sugar (page 234)

In a small bowl, beat the eggs and egg yolks with sugar, salt, lemon zest, 2 tablespoons olive oil, vanilla extract, and rum. Gradually add enough flour to form a rather soft dough. Turn out onto a floured surface and knead for a minute. Roll very thin. With a pastry cutter, a pizza cutter, or a very sharp knife, cut into strips 1 inch x 4 to 7 inches.

Slowly heat the oil in a small saucepan. Oil is at the right temperature when a small piece of dough dropped into it floats to the surface and begins to sizzle. Fry a few strips at a time, twirling them to give them odd shapes, until lightly golden. Drain and place on paper towels.

When all the ears are done, mound on a large serving plate, sprinkling each layer abundantly with vanilla-flavored confectioners sugar.

Yields 3 to 4 dozen.

P

PAN DI RAMERINO

ROSEMARY BUNS (P)

1 envelope active dry yeast
1 1/2 cups warm water
3/4 cup sugar
1 1/2 teaspoons salt
1/4 cup warm olive oil
6 cups unbleached flour
1/2 cup Malaga or Muscat raisins
1 tablespoon fresh or 1 teaspoon dry rosemary leaves
1 small egg, beaten with a pinch of salt

Dissolve the yeast in 1/2 cup of warm water with 1 teaspoon sugar and let rest until solution foams—3 to 5 minutes. Add the remaining cup of warm water, salt, oil, sugar, and enough flour to form a not-too-stiff dough. Turn out onto a floured surface and knead 3 minutes or until dough is smooth and elastic.

Spread the raisins and rosemary leaves over the work surface and knead the dough over them until all the raisins and rosemary have been incorporated. Divide into 12 parts and let rest for 5 minutes. Shape each part into a ball and line up on a lightly oiled and well floured baking sheet 2-3 inches apart. Cover with a towel and let rise in a warm place for 1 to 2 hours, or until buns have doubled in size.

Delicately brush the tops with the beaten egg, and bake in preheated 350 °F oven for 20 minutes or until the buns are nicely browned.

Yields 12.

PAN DI SPAGNA
SPONGE CAKE (P)

Pan di Spagna (bread of Spain) is a typical Jewish dessert. Its name derives probably from the fact that it was brought to other parts of Europe and to the Middle East by the refugees at the time of the Spanish Inquisition. It is a delicate dessert in its own right; however it is also very useful in the preparation of *dolci al cucchiaio*, desserts that must be eaten with a spoon, such as *Zuccotto*, an ice cream, or *Zuppe Inglese*. Tightly wrapped in plastic, it can be frozen for a long time, so that it is at hand when needed.

6 eggs, separated
1/2 teaspoon cream of Tartar
3/4 cup sugar
1 teaspoon vanilla extract
1/2 cup cake flour

Beat the egg whites with cream of Tartar until stiff peaks form. In a separate bowl beat the egg yolks with sugar until fluffy and lemon colored. Add vanilla extract and 1/4 of the beated egg whites. Mix well, then fold in the remaining egg whites.

Line a bread loaf pan with wax paper. Spoon the batter into it and bake in 350 °F oven for 45 minutes. Remove to cooling rack and wait until completely cool to unmold.

Serves 8.

PAN DI SPAGNA PER PESACH
PASSOVER SPONGE CAKE (P)

6 eggs, separated
1/8 teaspoon salt
1 cup sugar
1/4 cup fresh orange juice
1/2 cup Passover cake meal
1/4 cup potato starch
Freshly grated rind of 1 large lemon

In a small bowl, beat the egg whites with salt until soft peaks form.

In a larger bowl, place egg yolks, sugar, and orange juice and beat until frothy and lemon colored.

Combine the cake meal with the potato starch and the lemon zest. Gradually add to the egg-yolk mixture, beating until the batter is smooth, then fold in the egg whites.

Pour into an ungreased tube sponge-cake pan with removable bottom and bake in preheated 350 °F oven for 1 hour. Remove from oven and invert pan standing on its feet until cool before unmolding.

Serves 8 to 12.

PANETTONE
(D OR P)

2 envelopes active dry yeast
3/4 cup warm water
3/4 cup sugar
1 teaspoon salt
4 1/2 cups all-purpose flour
8 ounces (2 sticks) unsalted butter at room temperature
5 eggs
1 cup seedless dark (preferably Muscat) raisins
1/2 cup diced candied citron peel
2 teaspoons vanilla extract

In the large bowl of a mixer, dissolve 1 envelope of yeast in 1/2 cup warm water with 1 tablespoon sugar and 1 teaspoon salt. Add enough flour to make a batter the consistency of sour cream. When the batter begins to bubble—10-20 minutes—add the butter and the remaining sugar and beat until very smooth. Add the eggs one at a time, beating well after each addition. Dissolve the remaining yeast in the remaining 1/4 cup water with a pinch of sugar and add to the bowl. Add enough flour to make a rather thick batter and set aside for 2 hours or until more than doubled in bulk. Add the raisins, the candied citron peel, and the vanilla extract and mix until all is well amalgamated. Add enough flour to make a very soft dough.

Grease and line with wax paper a 7 inches across x 6 inches tall souffle dish (a tin cookie container by those dimensions would do), with the edge of the wax paper extending about 2 or 3 inches above the top of the dish. Transfer the dough to the baking dish, cover loosely with a damp cloth, and set aside for 2 hours or until the dough reaches the top of the pan (but not of the wax paper, since over leavening will result in a drop in the height of the panettone).

Place in a cold oven and set the temperature at 400 °F. After fifteen minutes lower the temperature to 350 °F and bake for another hour, or until a skewer inserted in the center comes out clean. Let cool for a while at room temperature, then unmold. Cool thoroughly on rack before storing in a plastic bag in cool, dry place.

Serves 12 or more.

NOTE: Panettone is an excellent, nutritious breakfast cake. To make it pareve to be served as a dessert with a meat meal, substitute pareve margarine or olive oil for butter. The flavor will be slightly different, but delightful nevertheless.

PANFORTE
FESTIVE FRUIT CAKE (P)

In a large skillet, place sugar, honey, cinnamon, cloves and vanilla extract. Bring to a boil and cook 3 minutes, stirring occasionally. Add almonds, citron peel and flour and remove from heat. Stir for a minute or so until all is well amalgamated.

Lightly oil and sprinkle with flour a 9-inch springform cake pan. Pour the mixture into it and flatten down with a spatula. Bake in preheated 350 °F oven for 5 minutes. Remove from heat and let cool at room temperature, then transfer to a serving dish and sprinkle abundantly with vanilla-flavored confectioners sugar.

Serves 6 to 8.

3/4 cup sugar
1/3 cup honey
1/2 teaspoon cinnamon
1/2 teaspoon cloves
1 teaspoon vanilla extract
2 cups whole almonds, unblanched
1/2 cup diced candied citron peel
2/3 cup unbleached flour
Vanilla-flavored sugar (page 234)

PASTA FROLLA
SHORT PASTRY (D)

This delicate pastry can be used to line the baking dish for any type of tart, but it is especially indicated for the delicious and delicate *Torta di Ricotta.*

Sift together flour and sugar. Add butter and egg yolk and mix just enough to get the dry ingredients moistened.

Make a ball and then roll it thin into a disk large enough to line a 10-inch tart dish. For future use, wrap the ball of pastry in wax paper and refrigerate.

Lines a 10-inch tart dish.

3/4 cup all-purpose flour
1/2 cup confectioners sugar
5 tablespoons butter, cut into small pieces
1 egg yolk

PASTA PER BORRICCHE E PASTICCINI

FLAKY DOUGH FOR TURNOVERS (P)

1 teaspoon salt
3/4 cup lukewarm water
1/4 cup vegetable oil
2 1/2 cups unbleached flour
1/2 cup pareve margarine, melted

Combine salt with water and oil. Add enough flour to make a rather soft dough. Knead 2 or 3 minutes; wrap in wax paper and set aside to rest, at room temperature, for approximately 30 minutes.

Place on a well-floured work surface and roll to 1/2- inch thickness, in a more or less rectangular shape, with the length three times the width. Brush the surface with margarine, lightly sprinkle with flour, and fold the long side into thirds. Wrap in wax paper and place in refrigerator for 20 minutes, or in freezer for 1 1/2 minutes.

Return to the floured surface and roll to 1/4-inch thickncss with the length three times the width. Brush with fat and sprinkle with flour. Fold again into thirds and place in freezer for 1 1/2 minutes. Repeat the rolling, brushing with fat, etc., three more times or until you have used all the margarine. Use as directed.

This pastry will make turnovers for 6.

PINOLATA
PINE NUT COOKIES (P)

1 egg or 2 egg whites
3/4 cup sugar
Small pinch salt
2 tablespoons orange juice
1 teaspoon almond extract
1 teaspoon vanilla extract
3/4 cup pinoli *(Italian pine nuts), slightly toasted*
1 cup unbleached flour
1 1/2 teaspoons baking powder

Beat egg with sugar and salt. Add orange juice, almond and vanilla extracts and half the pine nuts. Sift together flour and baking powder, add and mix.

Drop by the teaspoon over an oiled and floured baking sheet 2 inches apart. Sprinkle with the remaining pine nuts and bake in preheated 300 °F oven for 15 minutes. Let cool thoroughly on baking sheet before storing in cookie jar at room temperature.

Yields about 2 dozen.

PIZZARELLE COL MIELE
MATZA PANCAKES WITH HONEY (P)

8 regular matzot
5 eggs, slightly beaten
1/2 teaspoon salt
2 tablespoons shredded lemon rind
2 tablespoons brandy
1/2 cup chopped walnut meats
3/4 cup dark, seedless raisins
Olive oil
3/4 cup honey
3 tablespoons water
1 tablespoon lemon juice

Soak matzot in cold water for 1/2 hour or until softened through. Squeeze the water out. You should have 4 cups of firmly packed soaked matza. Combine with eggs, salt, lemon rind, brandy, nuts, and raisins.

Heat 1/3 cup of oil in a large skillet. Drop the matza mixture by the tablespoonful into it and fry over moderate heat, turning, until golden on both sides. Drain on paper towels. Continue to fry until you have used up all the mixture, adding oil to the pan as it becomes necessary.

Combine honey, water and lemon juice in a small saucepan. Bring to a boil and cook for 5 minutes. Arrange the pancakes on a serving plate and pour the honey syrup over them. Serve immediately.

Serves 6 to 8.

PIZZARELLE DI FARINA DOLCE
CHESTNUT-FLOUR PANCAKES (P OR D)

Serve these pancakes as a dessert, as a snack, as an unusual addition to a luncheon buffet, and, omitting the sugar and the cream, as a side dish to a roasted or broiled chicken.

3 cups chestnut flour
1/4 cup sugar
1/2 teaspoon salt
1/3 cup pinoli *(Italian pine nuts)*
1/2 cup dark seedless raisins
1 cup cold water
3 eggs, slightly beaten
Olive oil
1 cup heavy cream, whipped to soft peaks (optional)

Sift together chestnut flour, sugar and salt into a bowl. Add pinoli, raisins and water and stir until you have a smooth, thick batter. Add eggs and mix well.

Heat 1/3 cup oil in a medium skillet. Drop the mixture into it by the tablespoonful and fry until browned on both sides. Transfer to paper towels to drain. Continue to make pancakes, adding a tablespoon or two of fresh oil to the skillet as it becomes necessary. Serve at room temperature with or without the whipped cream.

Yields about 24.

PIZZA ROMANA
JEWISH FRUIT BARS (P)

Pizza Romana is an ancient dessert, created and used by the Roman Jews for family celebrations such as B'nei Mitzvah, Brith Milot, etc. Commercially it can still be found only in the Jewish bakery in the Roman Ghetto, where people from every part of the capital, and even from other places in Italy, go to buy it. The bakery is the last vestige of what was once the greatest conglomeration of Jewish specialty food shops in Italy. In the old days, it was cut into large diamonds and at the end of the festivities it was distributed among special members of the family (grandparents, great aunts and uncles, etc) to bring home. Nowadays, it is cut into small rectangles and I am not sure that the generous custom of giving them away still exists. The following is the authentic, original recipe.

6 cups unbleached flour
1 1/2 cups sugar
1 teaspoon salt
1 1/2 cups unblanched almonds, coarsely cut up
3/4 cup pinoli *(Italian pine nuts)*
1 cup dark, seedless raisins
3/4 cup diced candied citron peel
1 1/4 cups olive oil
1 cup dry white wine

Sift together flour, sugar, and salt into a large bowl. Add nuts and fruits and mix well. Add the oil and mix just until the ingredients are moistened. Add enough wine to make a solid pastry dough.

Spread over an ungreased 12"x18" baking sheet with low borders, and flatten down to an even thickness. With a long sharp knife score the pastry at equal distances—6 times lengthwise and 6 times widthwise—then cut through to obtain 49 rectangles.

Bake in preheated 400 °F oven for 30 minutes or until borders begin to look dark brown. Remove from the oven and let cool for a while before carefully transfering the pieces to a cooling rack (pizza romana is very brittle when hot). When thoroughly cool store in a cookie jar where it will keep for several weeks at room temperature.

Yields 49 pieces.

lou myers

RICCI DI CIOCCOLATA
CHOCOLATE CURLS (P OR D)

This is the simplest way of making chocolate decorations, and simple were indeed most desserts of the Italian Jews. Simple, however, applies only to the preparations and looks, because tastewise, their desserts are unsurpassable. If you want your curls to be pareve, you must use semisweet chocolate. For dairy desserts, I recommend milk chocolate which is more malleable.

1/2 pound block chocolate
Vegetable slicer or peeler

Keep the chocolate at room temperature, if your working room is 80 °F. If on the other hand the room temperature is at 68 or 70 degrees, you must keep the block a few seconds in a warm oven, or zap it for 3 seconds in the microwave oven. If the block is too hard, instead of curls you will get shavings; if it is too warm, it will not make curls but blobs.

When your block is at the ideal point (you will have to make a few trials before you reach the desired consistency) begin to pass the vegetable slicer or peeler over it, and let the curls drop on a piece of wax paper.

Store in airtight glass jars at room temperature until ready to use. Handle with care so as not to lose the shape. Use as directed.

RICCIARELLI DI SIENA
SIENA ALMOND COOKIES (P)

These cookies are a favorite at Purim and during Passover, and a welcome and exquisite dessert at any dinner party.

2 egg whites
Dash salt
Granulated sugar
Freshly grated rind of 1 orange
1 1/2 teaspoons almond extract
1 teaspoon vanilla extract
2 1/2 cups (10 ounces) finely chopped blanched almonds
1/2 cup Passover cake meal
Vanilla-flavored sugar (page 234)

Beat egg whites with salt until stiff and dry. Gradually add 1 cup sugar and beat until you have the consistency of marshmallow. Add the orange zest, almond and vanilla extracts, and finally add the almonds. Mix until you have a rather hard paste.

Combine the Passover cake meal with 1/4 cup sugar. Generously grease a baking sheet with the margarine and cover with the matza meal and sugar mixture.

Divide the almond paste into 24 to 30 equal parts and, with greased hands, shape each into a diamond. Place 2 inches apart on prepared baking sheet and bake in preheated 275 °F oven for 12 or 13 minutes.

Remove the cookies from the oven while they are still white and, while still hot, sprinkle abundantly with vanilla-flavored confectioners sugar, using a sifter. Carefully remove to a cooling rack. When completely cool, store in a tightly closed tin box at room temperature.

Yields 24 to 30.

RICOTTA UBRIACA
DRUNKEN RICOTTA (D)

Ricotta Ubriaca was one of my father's favorite desserts. It was made with finely-ground real coffee beans and Cognac, and because of these two ingredients we children were not allowed to have it. A version without coffee and brandy was what we had instead.

As an adult I tasted the original version and liked it very much, and I make it also with instant coffee powder.

1 pound whole milk ricotta
1/2 cup sugar
2 teaspoons finely ground espresso coffee beans or instant espresso
4 tablespoons brandy
2 tablespoons pinoli *(Italian pine nuts)*

Place ricotta in a colander over a container and let it drain in the refrigerator at least 24 hours. Transfer to a bowl, add the sugar, and mix with a wooden spoon until fluffy and smooth. Add coffee, stir a little (you don't want to stir too much if you use instant coffee), and place in refrigerator uncovered.

Moments before serving, remove from refrigerator, add brandy, and stir to combine. Spoon into small bowls or ramekins. Sprinkle with *pinoli* and serve.

Serves 6.

ROSCHETTE DOLCI

SWEET LITTLE RINGS (P)

1/4 cup olive oil
1/2 cup sugar
2 eggs
Grated rind of 1 lemon
1 tablespoon toasted sesame seeds
2 1/2 cups unbleached flour
1 1/2 teaspoons baking powder

Cream together oil and sugar. Add the eggs one at a time, beating after each addition. Add lemon zest and sesame seeds and mix. Sift together 1 cup flour and baking powder and add to the mixture; then add enough of the remaining flour to make a consistent dough.

Divide into 30 parts; roll each piece of dough with your hands to make 6-inch ropes. Join the two ends to form rings. Bake on an ungreased non-stick sheet in 350 °F oven for 10 minutes.

Yields 2 1/2 dozen.

ROSELLINE DI PURIM

PURIM ROSETTE (P)

Purim is the most joyous of the Jewish holidays which reminds us of a happy ending to an event that was potentially a tragic one. It is the holiday that provides the greatest opportunity for the display of artistry and patience in the preparation of a great number of different sweets to make this joyous holiday especially festive. Rosettes should be watched while being prepared by the expert, since the actual preparation is not as complicated as its description. My friend Wanda Caro of Florence has kindly done the demonstration for me. I subsequently have made *roselline* many times myself, and I will try to pass my knowledge along as best I can.

2 eggs
1 pinch salt
1 1/2 cups unbleached flour
1 1/2 cups olive oil for frying
1 1/2 cups honey

Slightly beat eggs and salt together. Gradually add enough flour to obtain a rather soft dough. Knead for 1 minute, then roll out with a rolling pin as thin as you can. With a pizza cutter or a very sharp knife, cut out approximately 24 strips 2 inches wide and 9 inches long. Fold each strip along the length in half, then pinch to close the open sides at 1 1/2-inch intervals. Loosely roll each strip on itself in a spiral pinching here and there so that it does not lose its shape. Fasten the outer end to prevent its opening while frying.

Heat the oil in a small saucepan until a piece of dough dropped into it sizzles immediately. Fry 1 rosette at a time until golden on both sides, turning only once. Hold a few seconds above the pan to drip, then gently place on a paper towel.

When all the rosettes are done, heat half the honey in a clean saucepan. As honey starts to bubble, dip 2 or 3 rosettes in it to coat. Remove to a serving plate, open-and-pinched sides up. Lower the heat and continue to dip the rosettes in the hot honey until they are all coated, gradually adding honey as necessary.

Yields about 24.

LouMyers

SALAME DI CIOCCOLATA I
CHOCOLATE SALAMI (P)

1 cup sugar
1/3 cup water
8 ounces semi-sweet baking chocolate, cut into chunks
3 tablespoons Alkermes (brightly-colored red liquor)
10 ounces unpeeled almonds or hazel nuts, toasted and finely powdered
1/4 cup diced candied citron peel
1/4 cup pinoli (*Italian pine nuts)*
1/2 cup unsweetened cocoa
1 tablespoon vanilla-flavored sugar (page 234)

Dissolve the sugar with water in a heavy-bottomed pan over high heat. When the mixture appears transparent (after 2 minutes or so), add the dark chocolate chunks, lower the heat and stir until the chocolate is melted—approximately 5 minutes. Remove from heat, add liquor, toasted nut powder, citron peel, and pine nuts and mix well.

Wait until the mixture has reached room temperature, to shape, with the help of a sheet of plastic wrap, into a 10-inch long cylinder to resemble a salami. Let rest several hours until quite firm. Spread cocoa and then confectioners sugar (without mixing) over a piece of wax paper, and roll the salami over it coating all sides. Store unwrapped in refrigerator for several hours then wrap it tightly. When almost ready to use leave for 30 minutes at room temperature, then cut slantwise into thin slices.

Serves 8.

SALAME DI CIOCCOLATA II
CHOCOLATE SALAMI II (D)

This salami, made with bread crumbs instead of nuts, is even more delicate than the one described in the preceding recipe. However, unlike that made with nuts and semisweet chocolate, this one is dairy and therefore not suitable for every type of meal.

1 cup fine plain bread crumbs
1/4 cup Alkermes (brightly colored red liquor)
3/4 cup sugar
1/4 cup milk
8 ounces fine milk chocolate cut into chunks
1/2 cup coarsely chopped candied citron peel
1/3 cup pinoli *(Italian pine nuts*
1/3 cup unsweetened cocoa
1 tablespoon vanilla-flavored sugar (page 234)

Place the bread crumbs in a bowl with the liquor and mix until they are all moistened with it.

Dissolve sugar with milk in a heavy-bottomed pan over moderate heat, stirring constantly. After 2 minutes, add the chocolate chips and keep on stirring until they are also dissolved (4 minutes or so). Remove from heat, add the bread mixture, citron peel and nuts and mix well to combine.

Wait until the mixture has reached room temperature to shape, with the aid of a piece of plastic wrap, into an 8-inch cylinder, to resemble a salami. Let rest until quite firm, then spread the cocoa over a piece of wax paper, sprinkle the confectioners sugar over it (without mixing) and roll the salami in it. Store, wrapped, in refrigerator. Leave 30 minutes at room temperature before thinly slicing it slantwise and serving.

Serves 8.

SALSA DI VINO
WINE SAUCE (P)

2 tablespoons pareve margarine
2 teaspoons potato starch
2 tablespoons sugar
2 cups dry white wine

Place the margarine and starch in a saucepan and cook, stirring, 1 or 2 minutes. Add sugar and wine and cook, stirring occasionally, another 5 minutes. Use on ice cream or as directed.

Yields 2 cups.

SAVOIARDI
LADY FINGERS (D OR P)

2 eggs, separated
1/4 teaspoon cream of tartar
Dash salt
1/2 cup sugar
3/4 cup cake flour
1/2 teaspoon baking powder
1 teaspoon freshly grated lemon rind
1/2 teaspoon vanilla extract
2 tablespoons butter or non-dairy margarine
1/4 cup unbleached flour

In a small bowl beat the egg whites with cream of tartar and salt until very dry.

In another small bowl beat the yolks with sugar until frothy and lemon colored.

Sift together flour and baking powder and gradually add to the beaten egg yolks while mixing. Add lemon zest and vanilla extract and mix well. Fold in the egg whites.

Grease a large baking sheet with butter (or margarine) and sprinkle with flour. Pour all the batter in a pastry bag with 1/2-inch aperture. Squeeze the bag, while twisting the top closed, over the baking sheet to form 3-inch strips. Place in preheated 325 °F oven for 13 minutes, or until fingers are slightly golden. Remove from heat and transfer to a wire rack to cool.

Yields approximately 3 dozen.

SCORZETTE DI ARANCE CANDITE

CANDIED ORANGE PEELS (P)

3 thick-skinned large oranges
Water
1 cup sugar
1/2 cup light corn syrup

Remove the "poles" from oranges and make a few cuts lengthwise to separate the peel from the pulp. Reserve the fruit for the Orange Jelly of page 113.

Cut the peel into small strips and place in a container with cold water. Let rest in refrigerator for 3 full days.

Drain and place in a saucepan with water to cover. Bring to a boil and cook 15 minutes, or until peel strips are soft. Drain.

Place in a skillet with sugar, corn syrup, and 1/4 cup water and bring to a boil. Lower heat and simmer until the syrup has become quite dense and almost entirely absorbed by the peels. Cool, then store in glass or plastic container in refrigerator.

Yields approximately 6 dozen.

SFRATTI

HONEY AND NUT STICKS (P)

Sfratti are the typical example of the symbolic origin of some Jewish desserts. The etymology of *sfratti* goes back to when the law that prevailed was the "law of the stick." When landlords could not collect from poor tenants, they would evict them with the persuasive aid of a stick. The same applied to the Jews of any status when they no longer were wanted in a community. In Italy the word sfratto, in fact, means eviction, and this marvelously tasting dessert looks just like the sticks used by those heartless landlords and by the enemies of the Jews.

3 cups unbleached flour
1 1/4 cups sugar
1/4 teaspoon salt
2/3 cup dry white wine
1/3 cup vegetable oil
1 cup honey
1/2 teaspoon cinnamon
1/2 teaspoon ground cloves
1/4 teaspoon black pepper
Dash ground nutmeg
Freshly ground rind of 1 orange
15 ounces walnut meats, chopped

Place flour, sugar and salt in a large bowl. Add wine and oil and quickly mix with your fingers or with a fork. Form into a ball, wrap in wax paper, and set aside in refrigerator.

In a large skillet, over high heat, bring the honey to a boil and cook for 3 minutes. Add the spices, orange zest, and nuts and cook another 5 minutes, stirring constantly. Remove the skillet from the heat and continue to stir until the mixture is cool enough to handle. Turn over onto a floured work surface and divide into 6 equal parts. Using your hands, roll each part into a cylindrical stick about 13 inches long. Then push it away from you.

Take the pastry dough from the refrigerator and divide it into 6 equal parts. With a small rolling pin, roll out each piece to form 4x14-inch strips. Place one stick of filling on each strip and wrap the dough around the filling, covering it completely. Pinch the ends closed. Place on a well-floured baking sheet, seam side down.

Bake in preheated 375 °F oven for 20 minutes. Remove from the baking sheet still warm, and wrap individually in aluminum foil. Leave at room temperature where sfratti keep fresh for several weeks. They actually taste better after they have been allowed to age for a few days. Just before serving, unwrap and cut slantwise into 1 1/2-inch sections.

Yields 6 sticks; 48 diamonds.

SPUMINI
LITTLE MERINGUE SHELLS (P)

I was never able to make *spumini* correctly until my cousin, Emma Finzi Servi, an excellent and sophisticated cook whom my mother, a refined cook herself, greatly admired, gave me the following recipe.

1 cup sugar
4 teaspoons baking powder
3 egg whites
pinch salt

Combine sugar and baking powder in a 2-cup measuring cup with a spout. Beat egg whites with salt until stiff and dry. Gradually add the sugar mixture and continue beating until stiff peaks form.

Lightly grease a cookie sheet and line it with baking paper. Drop the beaten mixture by the teaspoonful about 2 inches apart. Bake in preheated 225 °F oven for 1 hour, or until *spumini* are dry, but still white, or only slightly colored. Remove from oven.

Pick meringues one by one and push your thumb through the bottom to allow hot moisture to escape. Place again on the baking sheet upside down, turn the oven off and return the baking sheet to it, leaving the door ajar. Wait until they are thoroughly cool to store them in a clean, white pillow case until ready to use. Spumini can be served dry as part of a cookie platter (I like to serve them in combination with *moscardini* and Haman's Ears) or filled with whipped cream, as in next recipe.

Yields 3 to 4 dozen.

SPUMINI ALLA PANNA
WHIPPED-CREAM MERINGUE SANDWICHES (D)

1 pint heavy cream
3 dozen spumini *(see preceding recipe)*
1 1/2 dozen large paper cups (those used for cup cakes)

In a small bowl beat the cream until soft peaks form. Do not overbeat, lest it separates and eventually turns into butter if it is beaten beyond optimal point.

Place a spoonful of whipped cream over the hollowed part of a meringue shell. Press another shell gently over the cream and squeeze one side of each sandwich to form a "V". Place, squeezed side down, inside the paper cups.

Yields 18.

STRUDEL ALLE MANDORLE
STRUDEL WITH ALMOND FILLING (P)

8 ounces frozen Filo dough
1/4 cup pareve margarine, slightly melted
3 eggs, separated
Small pinch salt
2/3 cup sugar
1 1/2 cups blanched almonds, chopped fine
1 teaspoon vanilla extract
1/2 teaspoon almond extract
1 teaspoon freshly grated lemon rind
Vanilla-flavored sugar (page 234)

Prepare the Filo dough according to manufacturer's instructions brushing each layer with melted margarine. Set aside over a clean, dry cloth and cover with a damp cloth until ready with the filling.

Lightly beat the egg whites with salt and set aside. Beat the egg yolks with sugar until thick and lemon colored. Add the almonds, vanilla and almond extracts, lemon zest, and egg white and mix well with a spatula.

Remove the damp cloth from the prepared Filo dough and spread the filling over it, leaving a margin of 1-inch all around. With the help of the cloth underneath, roll the dough as for a jelly roll, and pinch the ends closed to prevent the filling from escaping.

Place seam side down on ungreased baking sheet, carefully poke holes with the pointy tip of a sharp knife all over the top, then brush with melted margarine. Bake in preheated 375 °F oven for 30 minutes. Remove from heat and sprinkle with vanilla-flavored confectioners sugar. Serve at room temperature.

Serves 6.

STRUDEL ALLE MELE

STRUDEL WITH APPLE FILLING (P)

2 cups unbleached flour
1/4 cup whole wheat flour
3/4 cup sugar
1/2 teaspoon salt
3/4 cup warm olive oil or melted pareve margarine
1 egg
1 cup warm water
3 pounds good cooking apples
2 1/2 teaspoons ground cinnamon
2 tablespoons brandy
1/4 cup fine unflavored bread crumbs
1/4 cup white seedless raisins
1/4 cup chopped walnut meats
4 tablespoons orange jelly (page 113)
Vanilla-flavored sugar (page 234)

Mix together the two flours, 1/4 cup sugar, salt, 1/2 cup oil or margarine, egg, and enough warm water to form a dough that is neither too stiff nor too soft. Knead it over a floured surface until very smooth and elastic, then make a ball and place in an oiled warmed bowl, cover with a damp warm cloth and let it rest in a warm place for 45 minutes to 1 hour.

Pare the apples, remove the core, and cut into thin slices. Place in a bowl with the cinnamon, brandy, and the remaining 1/2 cup sugar and toss to mix.

In a small frying pan heat the remaining oil or margarine and saute the bread crumbs in it.

Turn the dough over a floured cloth and with a rolling pin roll it down as thin as you can. Spread the bread crumbs over it. Add the apple slices and flatten with a spatula, leaving a margin of 1-inch all around. Sprinkle with raisins and chopped nuts and place a dollop of gelatine here and there.

With the help of the cloth, roll the dough as for a jelly roll, and pinch the ends closed to prevent the filling from escaping. Place seam side down on a greased and floured baking sheet, brush with oil or melted margarine, and bake in preheated 350 °F oven for 45 minutes. Remove from heat and sprinkle with vanilla-flavored confectioners sugar. Serve warm or at room temperature.

Serves 6.

NOTE: You can make a strudel with practically any fruit. Just substitute apples with your favorite fruits—fresh or dry—and proceed as above. For easier control, make two small rolls instead of a large one.

STRUFOLI DI PURIM

PURIM STRUFOLI (P)

2 eggs
2 egg yolks
1/4 cup sugar
1/2 teaspoon salt
3 tablespoons olive oil
1 teaspoon anise seeds
2 1/2 cups unbleached flour
1 cup or more oil for frying
Honey

Beat together eggs, egg yolks, sugar, salt, olive oil, and anise seeds. Add enough flour to make a rather consistent dough. Roll it thin and cut into strips 1/2x10 inches.

Heat the oil in a small saucepan where it stays a couple of inches deep. Knot the strips loosely to form "airy" balls, and fry in the hot oil one or two at a time. Drain thoroughly over paper towels. When cool, drizzle some honey over them and serve.

Yields approximately 2 dozen.

T

TAGLIATELLE DOLCI IN FORNO
SWEET NOODLE PUDDING (D)

We learned to make this dish from a family of Polish refugees who were confined in our village during WWII. Of course we made our own pasta and used ricotta which was readily available. However, now fresh pasta can be bought practically in any grocery store, and ricotta can be substituted with cottage cheese, as the original recipe required. Whichever your preference, you can serve this as a side dish, as part of a brunch, or as a nutritious dessert.

3 large baking apples
3/4 cup seedless raisins
1/2 cup sugar
1 teaspoon ground cinnamon
2 tablespoons rum
1 tablespoon honey
2 eggs
2 egg yolks
1 pint ricotta or cottage cheese
1 cup whole milk
1/2 pound fresh egg tagliatelle or fettuccine
1 tablespoon salt
6 tablespoons sweet butter
Unseasoned fine bread or cookie crumbs

Core and pare the apples and cut into slices. Place in a bowl with raisins, 1/4 cup sugar, cinnamon, rum, and honey. Toss and let marinate for a few hours or overnight in refrigerator.

In a large bowl beat eggs and egg yolks with 1/4 cup sugar. Add ricotta and mix well until smooth. Add milk and stir to combine.

Cook fettuccine in 3 quarts of boiling water with a tablespoon salt for 3 minutes. Drain not too dry and place in a large bowl with 4 tablespoons butter and toss.

Grease with butter and dust with crumbs a 13x8-inch baking dish. Transfer 1/3 of the tagliatelle into it, then half the apples, another third of tagliatelle, the remaining apples and lastly the remaining tagliatelle. Dot with butter and bake in 350 °F oven for 45 minutes. Serve hot or at room temperature.

Serves 8.

TAIGLACH FOR PESACH
(P)

Taiglach is very similar to the Italian *Ceciarchiata*. But whereas in Italy we served *ceciarchiata*, cut into segments, mainly at Purim and at Rosh Hashanah, Grandmother Raizel, an Ashkenazi, served Taiglach in mounds, to be picked with your fingers, exclusively at Pesach.

3 eggs, slightly beaten
1/2 teaspoon salt
2 1/2 cups fine matza meal
1 1/2 cups honey
1 teaspoon ground ginger root
1/2 cup hazelnuts
1/2 cup mixed candied fruit

Combine eggs and salt and add enough matza meal to make a rather soft dough. Turn out on a work surface and knead a minute or two. Shape into a few ropes 1/2 inch in diameter. With a sharp knife, cut the ropes into 1/2-inch pieces.

Place loosely on an ungreased baking sheet and bake in preheated 400 °F oven for 7 minutes.

Bring the honey to a boil and cook over moderately high heat for 3 minutes. Add ginger, the baked pieces of dough, the hazel nuts and candied fruit, and cook over low heat 5 minutes longer, stirring often.

Empty the hot mixture over three dishes forming three mounds and let cool to room temperature. Place the dishes at three strategic points on the table, and let people pick the honied pieces with their own fingers. Messy but a lot of fun!

Serves 8 to 12.

TIRAMISU
(D)

Tirami su means, literally, "pull me up." And in fact this rich, delicious, yet delicate dessert was once used to give convalescent people a new strength. Many, many years ago (I was a child of seven), while Mother was recovering from an illness, our maid made *tirami su* every day and that's when I learned to love it.

In recent years *tiramisu* (now spelled as one word) has made a triumphal comeback and has become a household name both in Italy and in America, and a favorite at fine restaurants.

- *1 pound mascarpone cheese*
- *1/4 cup vanilla-flavored sugar (page 234)*
- Crema pasticcera *(page 83)*
- *36 lady fingers*
- *1/4 cup rum or other liqueur you favor*
- *1/4 cup espresso coffee*
- *4 ounces milk chocolate, melted*
- *2/3 cup milk chocolate shavings (page 179) or 1/3 cup unsweetened cocoa*

Have all the ingredients at room temperature. Gently mix mascarpone and sugar with a rubber spatula. Add *crema pasticcera* a little at a time and keep on stirring by hand until all is amalgamated.

Place 12 lady fingers at the bottom of a square or rectangular oven-to-table dish. Mix liqueur and coffee and drizzle the cookies with 1/3 the mixture, cover with 1/3 the mascarpone mixture, and sprinkle with 1/2 the melted chocolate.

Repeat layering in the same order, covering the top with chocolate shavings or, in default of those, with unsweetened cocoa. Place in refrigerator until ready to serve.

Serves 8 or more.

TORRONE ALLE MANDORLE
ALMOND NOUGAT (P)

2 egg whites
1/2 cup honey
1 cup sugar
1/3 cup water
3 cups blanched whole almonds
1 tablespoon chopped candied orange peel
1 teaspoon vanilla extract
1 teaspoon freshly grated lemon rind

Beat the egg whites until stiff peaks form.

Place the honey in a large skillet; place the sugar and water in a small saucepan. Bring both to a boil and let honey cook 3 minutes; then lower the heat to a minimum. Let sugar syrup boil for 5 minutes or until a drop lifted with a small spoon falls back into the pan forming a "thread" . Turn off the heat under the sugar syrup.

Add the beaten egg whites to the honey skillet while stirring constantly, and as soon as the mixture is free of lumps, gradually add the sugar syrup. Add the almonds, candied orange peel, vanilla extract, and lemon zest. Turn the heat off and mix to combine.

Pour the hot mixture into a 15 x 4 inches loaf pan, lined with wax paper. Allow to cool thoroughly, then unmold, peel off the wax paper and cut into sticks 1 inch wide.

Yields 15 individual torroni.

TORTA AL MASCARPONE
MASCARPONE CHEESE CAKE (D)

3 eggs, separated
9 tablespoons sugar
1 pound mascarpone cheese, at room temperature
40 Biscottini di Rona, *or vanilla cookies*
3/4 cup cold strong coffee
2 tablespoons rum
*1/4 cup sugar-toasted chopped almonds**

Beat egg whites until stiff peaks form. Gradually add half the sugar and beat until mixture has the consistency of marshmallow.

In another bowl, beat the egg yolks with the remaining sugar until frothy and lemon-colored. Reduce the speed, add the cheese, and beat until well mixed. Add the whites and mix well.

Mix together rum and coffee. In a serving bowl, make alternate layers of cheese mixture and cookies quickly dipped in the coffee mixture, ending with the cheese.

Sprinkle the top with toasted almonds and chill at least 1 hour before serving.

Serves 6 or more.

*To make sugar-coated toasted almonds, place the chopped almonds in a small skillet with 2 tablespoons sugar, 2 tablespoons water, 1 teaspoon almond extract. Bring to a boil and cook, stirring, for 2 to 3 minutes, or until almonds are dry and light brown. Remove from heat and stir until cool.

NOTE: This is exactly the way we made *Torta al Mascarpone.* If you don't think you can trust raw eggs, however, you'd be better off making the Tiramisu' of page 201 which is a variation of the above.

TORTA BUONA DELLA MAMMA

MAMMA'S GOOD CAKE (D OR P)

This is an all-occasion cake, good, to be sure, whether you make it with milk or orange juice. With milk it results in a somewhat more delicate cake; with orange juice, however, it has the advantage of being pareve—a desirable feature especially if served in a festive meal, which is likely to include meat dishes.

1 stick butter or pareve margarine.
1 pinch salt
Sugar
3 eggs
2 1/2 to 3 cups cake flour
2 1/2 teaspoons baking powder
2 teaspoons vanilla extract
1 cup milk or orange juice
1/4 cup diced candied citron peel
1/2 cup chocolate chips
1/2 cup whole blanched almonds

Cream together butter, salt and 1 cup sugar. Add eggs one at a time, beating after each addition.

Sift together 2 cups of flour and the baking powder; add to the egg mixture, alternating with milk or orange juice and 1 teaspoon vanilla extract. Add candied citron peel and chocolate chips and enough of the remaining flour to form a consistent batter.

Pour into a 10-inch springform cake pan greased and dusted with a mixture of flour and sugar. Spread the almonds over the top, and place immediately in a preheated 350 °F oven. Bake for 45 minutes or until a knife blade inserted at center comes out clean.

In the meantime mix 1/2 cup sugar with 1 teaspoon vanilla extract and 2 tablespoons milk or orange juice.

Remove from oven and brush the top with the sugar mixture while still very hot. Allow to cool thoroughly before unmolding and serving.

Serves 12.

TORTA DEL RE
KING'S CAKE (P OR D)

I gave this cake the name "King's Cake" because according to a family story it came from the secret recipe files of the pastry chef of the king of Italy, Vittorio Emanuele III.

As a young woman my mother's aunt, Flora, was the tutor of the child of Senator Mosconi of Vicenza, whose wife was bedridden. In addition to tutoring the child, the young woman was also apparently consoling the senator, because one day she found herself pregnant. Since this could not be tolerated in her family, she jumped from the window of her third-floor apartment (which in Italy is pretty high) with the intent of taking her own life. But she didn't die, and while she was recovering from a few broken bones, the senator's wife died and the senator married my great aunt, thus saving her honor.

My mother, as a young lady, was often invited to this aunt's house for dinner when this cake was served, and she heard over and over again from the mouth of Donna Flora herself, that the recipe for it had been given to the senator's chef by his friend, the king's chef. Eventually, as an adult, my mother was able to obtain the recipe, which she made for her family on very special occasions.

This is a true story, and not only did I choose to call it "King's Cake" for the reason I mentioned, but also because it is "fit for a king" and it is my piece de resistance for important dinners and at Passover.

2 tablespoons pareve [Passover] margarine or butter
2 tablespoons matza meal or bread

Grease and sprinkle with bread crumbs or matza meal a 10-inch springform cake pan and set aside.

Beat the egg whites with salt until stiff and dry.

In a larger bowl, beat the egg yolks with sugar until

crumbs
5 eggs, separated
1 pinch of salt
1 1/4 cups sugar
2 1/2 cups (10 ounces) blanched almonds, chopped fine
1 teaspoon vanilla extract
1 teaspoon almond extract
Grated rind of 1 lemon
Vanilla-flavored sugar (page 234)
Sliced almonds, toasted

lemon colored. Gradually add the chopped almonds, then the two extracts and the lemon zest. You should have a very hard paste. Mix 1/3 of the beaten egg white with the almond mixture to make it softer. Delicately fold in the remaining egg white and pour into the prepared cake pan.

Place in the center of a middle rack in preheated 325 °F oven and bake for 1 hour without ever opening the oven door. After the hour is over, turn the heat off and leave the oven door ajar for 10 to 15 minutes; then remove the pan from the oven and invert on a cooling rack. When the cake is thoroughly cool, remove it from the pan and place it upside down on a cake dish. Top with vanilla-flavored confectioners sugar, using a sifter, and sprinkle with toasted sliced almonds.

Serves 12.

TORTA DI AZZIMA PESTA
MATZA MEAL CAKE (P)

Passover pareve margarine
2 3/4 cups matza meal
5 eggs, separated
1/2 teaspoon salt
1 cup sugar
grated rind of 1 lemon
1 teaspoon vanilla extract
1/4 cup vanilla-flavored sugar (page 234)

Coat bottom and sides of an 8-inch springform cake pan with margarine, then sprinkle with matza meal.

In a small bowl beat egg whites with salt until stiff and dry, and set aside. In a larger bowl beat yolks with sugar until lemon colored. Add 2 1/2 cups of matza meal, lemon zest, and vanilla extract. Delicately fold in the beaten egg whites.

Pour into the prepared cake pan and immediately place at center rack of a preheated 350 °F oven for 45 minutes, or until a skewer inserted in center comes out dry.

Remove from oven and let stand on cooling rack upside down until cool. Unmold inverted over a cake plate and sprinkle abundantly with vanilla-flavored confectioners sugar.

Serves 8.

TORTA DI CIOCCOLATA E ALBUMI

CHOCOLATE EGG-WHITE CAKE (P)

This recipe was first conceived when the craze about eliminating egg yolks from one's diet had not yet reached the present proportions. Most recipes then called for egg yolks rather than whole eggs and people often wondered what to do with the whites. This cake answers the question since it is made with only whites. Egg whites can be frozen and accumulated by adding them to the jar in the freezer as they become available. When ready to use them, defrost the whole jar and measure with a cup, then refreeze. Keep in mind that 1 cup is equivalent to 8 whites.

8 egg whites (1 cup)
1/2 teaspoon salt (scant)
1/2 cup unsweetened cocoa powder
1 cup sugar
3 tablespoons vegetable oil
1/3 cup hazelnuts, toasted and coarsely chopped
1/3 cup almonds, toasted and coarsely chopped
1/3 cup finely chopped walnut meats
Semisweet chocolate curls (page 179) or Vanilla-flavored sugar (page 234)

Beat 6 egg whites with salt until dry and set aside.

Combine the cocoa with sugar, oil and the remaining unbeaten egg whites in a large bowl. Add the nuts and mix well. Add 1/4 of the beaten whites and mix again. Fold in the remaining beaten whites and pour into an oiled and lightly floured 9-inch cake pan.

Bake in preheated 350 °F oven for approximately 30 minutes. The cake is done when a skewer inserted in the center of it comes out dry. Transfer to a wire rack to cool. Invert over a cake dish and cover with chocolate curls or sprinkle abundantly with vanilla-flavored confectioners sugar.

Serves 8.

TORTA DI CIOCCOLATA PER PESACH

PASSOVER CHOCOLATE CAKE (P)

6 tablespoons Passover pareve margarine
2 tablespoons fine matza meal
4 ounces unsweetened baking chocolate, coarsely chopped
1 tablespoon instant dark coffee powder
5 eggs, separated
1 pinch salt
1 cup sugar
1 1/4 cups finely ground toasted almonds
1 teaspoon vanilla extract
Freshly grated rind of 1 orange
3/4 cup toasted and coarsely chopped hazel nuts
4 ounces non-dairy semi-sweet chocolate chips
3 tablespoons unsweetened cocoa

Grease a 9-inch springform cake pan with 2 tablespoons margarine, sprinkle with matza meal and invert to remove excess.

Melt the unsweetened chocolate with the remaining 4 tablespoons margarine in a heavy saucepan over low heat. Add the dry instant coffee and stir until all is well amalgamated.

Beat egg whites with salt in a small bowl until stiff and dry. In a larger bowl, beat egg yolks with sugar until thick and lemon colored. Decrease the speed and gradually add the melted chocolate, almonds, vanilla extract, orange zest, and one third of the beaten egg white. Add the hazel nuts and chocolate chips and mix to combine.

Delicately fold in the remaining egg white and pour into the prepared cake pan. Bake in preheated 325 °F oven for 45 minutes, then turn the heat off, open the door ajar, and allow the cake to cool inside for 10 minutes. Remove from oven and let cool thoroughly on a wire rack before inverting the cake over a serving dish. Brush off the loose matza meal and sprinkle with cocoa.

Serves 12.

TORTA DI INES
INES'S CAKE (D)

A slice of this simple and delicious cake, a dollop of homemade vanilla ice cream, and a small glass of sweet vermouth were the only refreshments served on the day of my Bat Mitzvah—June 5, 1938 (Shavu'ot 5698).

3/4 cup granulated sugar
6 tablespoons soft butter
3 eggs
1/2 teaspoon vanilla extract
Grated rind of 1 lemon
1 1/2 cups cake flour
1 teaspoon baking soda
3 teaspoons cream of tartar
1/2 cup milk
Milk chocolate curls (page 179) or Vanilla-flavored sugar (page 234)

Cream together sugar and butter. Add the eggs, one at a time, beating after each addition. While beating, add vanilla extract and lemon zest. Gradually add the flour and beat just enough for the batter to be smooth.

Combine the baking soda and the cream of tartar in a cup and stir, adding the milk while stirring. The mixture will foam and expand. When it is about to overflow from the cup, pour into the bowl with the batter, and quickly stir until the batter is smooth again.

Pour into a buttered and lightly floured 9-inch cake pan and bake in preheated 350 °F oven for 35 to 40 minutes, or until straw inserted at center of cake comes out dry. Remove from oven and let cool on a wire rack for 1/2 hour. Turn upside down on a cake dish and cover with milk chocolate curls or sprinkle with vanilla-flavored confectioners sugar.

Serves 8 or more.

TORTA DI MELE
APPLE CAKE (P)

4 large cooking apples
1 1/2 cups sugar
1 teaspoon cinnamon
1 tablespoon rum
1/2 cup vegetable oil
1 tablespoon honey
3 eggs
1 cup orange juice
1 teaspoon vanilla extract
3 cups unbleached flour
2 teaspoons baking powder

Pare and core apples, then cut into not-too-thin slices. Place in a bowl with 2 tablespoons sugar, the cinnamon, and the rum, and toss to mix. Set aside.

Cream together oil, sugar and honey. Add the eggs one at a time, beating after each addition.

Mix together orange juice and vanilla extract. Mix together flour and baking powder. Add to the bowl a bit at a time, alternating the juice with the dry mixture.

Turn 1/3 of the batter into a 10-inch oiled and floured springform cake pan; spread 1/2 of the marinated apples over the batter, then another 1/3 of batter, the remaining apples, and lastly the remaining batter.

Bake in a preheated 350 °F oven for 1 1/2 hours or until a skewer inserted at center comes out clean. Serve at room temperature.

Serves 12.

TORTA DI NOCI PER PESACH
PASSOVER WALNUT CAKE (P)

2 tablespoons Passover pareve margarine
3 tablespoons matza meal
2 1/2 cups (10 ounces) choice walnut meats
6 eggs, separated
1/8 teaspoon salt
1 1/2 cups granulated

Grease a 10-inch springform cake pan with margarine, sprinkle with matza meal, and invert to remove excess. Place the walnut meats in the work bowl of a processor fitted with the metal blade, and process until chopped fine—10 to 13 seconds.

Beat the egg whites with salt until stiff and dry. In a large bowl beat the egg yolks with sugar until thick and lemon colored. Gradually add the finely ground walnut meats and one fourth of the beaten egg white. Add orange zest, honey, vanilla extract, cinnamon, and cloves and mix to combine.

Delicately fold in the remaining egg white, then spoon into the prepared cake pan. Place at the center of middle rack in preheated 325 °F oven and bake for 1 hour without opening the oven door. When the hour is over, test with a skewer at center, and if it comes out dry the cake is done; otherwise bake for another 10 or 15 minutes. Remove from oven and invert over a cooling rack. Allow to cool thoroughly before unmolding upside down over a cake dish. Using a sifter, lightly sprinkle with vanilla-flavored confectioners sugar.

Serves 12 or more.

sugar
Grated rind of 1 orange
1 teaspoon honey
1/2 teaspoon vanilla extract
1/2 teaspoon cinnamon
1/4 teaspoon ground cloves
Vanilla-flavored sugar (page 234)

TORTA DI PERE
PEAR TART (P)

Place the pears in a bowl with all the other ingredients, except for the *Pasta Frolla*, toss and let marinate for a few hours. Roll the pastry thin and line a 10-inch baking dish with it. Add the pears and their liquid and bake at 350 °F for 45 minutes.

Serves 8.

2 pounds Bosc pears, peeled, cored and sliced
2 tablespoons sugar
2 tablespoons brandy
1/4 teaspoon cinnamon
1/4 teaspoon grated orange peel
1 recipe Pasta Frolla

TORTA DI RICOTTA
RICOTTA TART (D)

1 1/2 pounds whole milk or part skim ricotta
Pasta Frolla
1 egg
3 egg yolks
1/2 cup sugar
The grated rind of 1 orange
The grated rind of 1 lemon
1 teaspoon vanilla extract
Vanilla-flavored sugar (page 234)

Keep the ricotta in a colander over a container in the refrigerator for several days or at least overnight, to rid it of excess moisture.

Roll the pastry thin and line with it your most elegant, oven-to-table 10-inch tart dish.

Beat together ricotta, egg, egg yolks, sugar, orange and lemon rind, and vanilla extract. until fluffy and smooth. Spoon into the lined baking dish.

Bake in preheated 350 °F oven for 45 minutes, or until a skewer inserted at center comes out somewhat dry.

Remove from oven and place on a cooling rack. Wait until the last moment to sift confectioners sugar over it and serve. (If you cover it with sugar too soon, the inevitable moisture will matt the sugar; its taste will be the same, but its appearance will be much less elegant.)

Serves 12.

TORTA MARCELLA
MARCELLA'S CAKE (P)

My sister Marcella is a great cook, but her real strength lies in baking. She created this cake when her children were small and, with slight variations, she served it either for breakfast (with raisins) or for dessert (with chocolate chips) almost every day.

1/2 pound (2 sticks) pareve margarine, at room temperature
1 1/2 cups sugar
5 eggs
The rind of 1 lemon
1/2 cup orange juice
1 teaspoon vanilla extract
1 cup chopped almonds or walnuts
1 cup raisins or chocolate chips
2 cups unbleached flour
1 teaspoon salt
2 teaspoons baking powder

Reserve 2 tablespoons of margarine and cream the rest with sugar in a large bowl. Add the eggs one at a time, beating after each addition. Chop the lemon rind in a blender with 1/2 cup orange juice and add to the bowl. Add vanilla extract, nuts and raisins or chocolate chips.

Sift together flour, salt and baking powder. Lower the speed and gradually add the flour mixture to the bowl.

With the reserved margarine grease a 13x8-inch baking pan and dust with flour. Pour the batter into it and bake in 375 °F oven for 45 minutes.

Serves 12.

NOTE: When Marcella created this cake, the food processor had not yet been invented. But even if you own one it is preferable to use a blender with some juice to chop lemon or orange rind. If using a processor, cut the rind into 2 to 3-inch strips and process together with 1/3 of the sugar in the recipe. Of course you can always manually grate or chop the rind.

TORTA TUNISINA
TUNISIAN ICE CREAM CAKE (D)

3 eggs
1 cup granulated sugar
3/4 pound unsalted butter at room temperature
1 1/2 teaspoons vanilla extract
70 or 80 sweet tea biscuits
1 1/4 cups strong espresso, laced with
3 tablespoons brandy

Beat together eggs and sugar until thick and lemon colored. Add butter, one third at a time, beating until the cream is light and fluffy. Add vanilla extract and mix.

Line the walls and bottom of a glass bowl with biscuits quickly dipped in the coffee mixture. Pour some of the cream inside the lined bowl, cover with biscuits dipped in the coffee and keep on making layers alternating coffee-dipped biscuits and cream until all the ingredients are used up. Cover the bowl with plastic wrap, then aluminum foil and place in the freezer for at least a few hours before serving.

With the warmed blade of a knife, separate the ice cream from the walls of the bowl, and after a few minutes unmold upside down over a cake dish. Serve immediately.

Serves 12.

TORTELLI DOLCI DI SHAVUOT
SWEET SHAVUOT TORTELLI (D)

1 1/2 cups ricotta
2 egg yolks
Sugar
2 tablespoons minced candied citron peel
2 tablespoons pinoli *(Italian pine nuts)*
1/2 teaspoon vanilla extract
2 cups unbleached flour
1/2 teaspoon salt
2 eggs
3 tablespoons vegetable oil
2 tablespoons rum or brandy
1/2 teaspoon freshly grated lemon rind
Vanilla-flavored sugar (page 234)

In a large skillet heat the ricotta and stir until most moisture has evaporated. Let cool a little, then combine with 1 egg yolk, 3 tablespoons sugar, citron peel, pinoli and vanilla extract; mix well and set aside in refrigerator.

Make a soft dough with the flour, salt, eggs, the remaining egg yolk, 1/4 cup sugar, oil, rum, and lemon zest. Knead for 3 minutes, then cover with a clean towel and let rest for 5 minutes. With a manual pasta machine or with a rolling pin roll the pastry thin. Cut into disks with a round cookie cutter or a wine glass about 3 inches in diameter.

Place 1 teaspoonful of ricotta mixture off center on each disk. Fold over in half and press the round edge with the prongs of a fork to seal. Poke a few holes on the tops, place tortelli on an ungreased baking sheet, and bake in preheated 350 °F oven for 25 minutes. Sprinkle with vanilla-flavored confectioners sugar and serve.

Yields about 3 dozen.

TORZETTI DELL'ABBREI
HARD COOKIES OF THE JEWS (P)

Torzetti and *Marroncini* were specialties of Pitigliano made for holidays as well as for family celebrations. When as a married woman living in the United States I went to Pitigliano to learn from my old aunt how to make them, she regretfully told me that she didn't remember because she had not made them in decades. No written recipes had ever existed; both were handed down from generation to generation by word of mouth and observation. I never had seen them made, because Mother, being from Rome, preferred to have her sisters-in-law make the Pitigliano specialties for our family and to reciprocate with her Roman ones. However, my aunt told me, one of the public bakers was making them much like the originals. I went to interview the baker—an intelligent young Christian woman—and I found out to my amusement that she had bestowed on them the attribute *dell'abbrei*, the way of saying "of the Jews" in the Pitiglianese dialect.

I asked her how she knew about *torzetti* and she told me this interesting story: She had learned to make them from *La Bafifa*, the old woman who had been our baker for over half a century. The old woman was so jealous of the treasured recipes she had learned from the Jews that she was very reluctant to share them with anyone. Only after a lot of pressure from the young apprentice had she finally agreed to show her how to make *torzetti*. However, she withheld one detail. When the moment came to test the sugar, the old woman held her large apron high, as a screen to block the other's view. It took a lot of begging to win the old woman's heart, but at last the young baker gained the skill that would otherwise have been lost. (None of my cousins remembered how to make *Torzetti* or *Marroncini*, although I stirred up a world of beautiful memories when I mentioned them.)

The young baker kindly invited us to watch her while she made them. So, while I paid careful attention, and my husband stood ready with paper and pen, we recorded two of the oldest Italian-Jewish dessert recipes. Typical of the generosity of the Pitiglianesi and their long-standing friendship with the Jews, after the cookies were baked, the young woman insisted that we take all of them as a gift. Since in Pitigliano there are no Jews left, she bakes them for her Christian customers only around Christmas, she said. These were made—in the middle of the summer—expressly for me and my family!

Combine flour, baking powder, cloves, and orange and lemon zest. Mound on a work surface (or in a large bowl) and make a well in the center.

Place the sugar with 1 cup of cold water in a saucepan and bring to a boil. When the solution begins to reach full boil, start stirring with a wooden spoon. After 3 minutes, begin to test for the ideal cooking point of the syrup, which comes when a drop held between thumb and forefinger, in an opening and closing motion, forms a thread at the fourth opening.

Pour all the hot syrup at the center of the well. Quickly mix in the flour mixture and knead while the dough that forms is still hot. With a rolling pin roll down to 1/2-inch thickness. Cut into 2-inch-tall diamonds with a sharp knife; then coat the diamonds all over with the leftover flour mixture.

Place on a well-floured baking sheet and bake in preheated 400 °F oven for 10 to 12 minutes. If everything went well, *torzetti* should be slightly less white and each should have formed a bubble of air at the center.

Yields about 50.

3 cups unbleached flour
*1/2 teaspoon ammonium bicarbonate**
or
1 teaspoon baking powder
1 teaspoon ground cloves
Grated rind of 1 orange
Grated rind of 1 lemon
1 1/4 cups sugar
1 cup cold water

*Ammonium bicarbonate can be purchased from pharmacies. It is *not* the same as sodium bicarbonate (baking soda) available in supermarkets.

U

UOVA DI CIOCCOLATA
CHOCOLATE EGGS (D)

3/4 pound hazelnuts or filberts
8 ounces finest milk chocolate, coarsely chopped
2 teaspoons vanilla extract
1 pound semisweet chocolate, coarsely chopped
1 tablespoon unsalted butter

Toast the nuts until the peels are black. As soon as can be handled peel them by rubbing a few at a time between the palms of your hands. Chop nuts fine.

In a heavy-bottomed pan, over low heat, place the milk chocolate and vanilla extract and stir until chocolate is barely melted. Remove from heat, add chopped nuts and mix well. Let cool for a while.

Take a spoonfull of the mixture at a time and with your buttered hands shape an egg and set on a piece of wax paper to cool completely.

Place the semisweet chocolate and 1 tablespoon of butter into a clean heavy-bottomed pan and stir over very low heat until the chocolate is completely melted, then remove from heat. Take one egg at a time and dip into the melted chocolate and place on a piece of wax paper to solidify. Leave at room temperature for one whole day before storing in a cookie jar at room temperature, where they remain fresh for several weeks.

Yields 1 dozen.

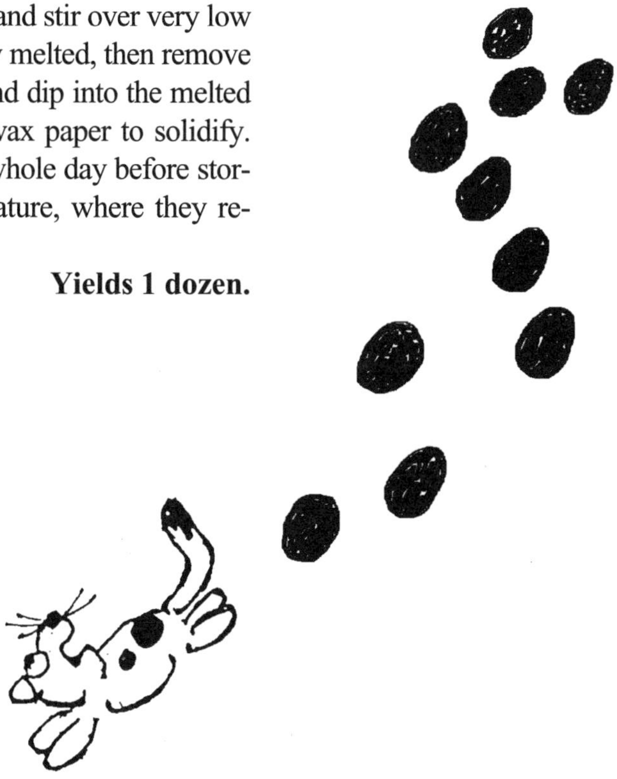

UOVA DI NEVE
SNOW EGGS (D)

4 cups milk
3 2x1/2-inch strips of lemon peel
6 eggs, separated
Small pinch of salt
1/4 cup vanilla-flavored sugar (page 234)
3/4 cup granulated sugar

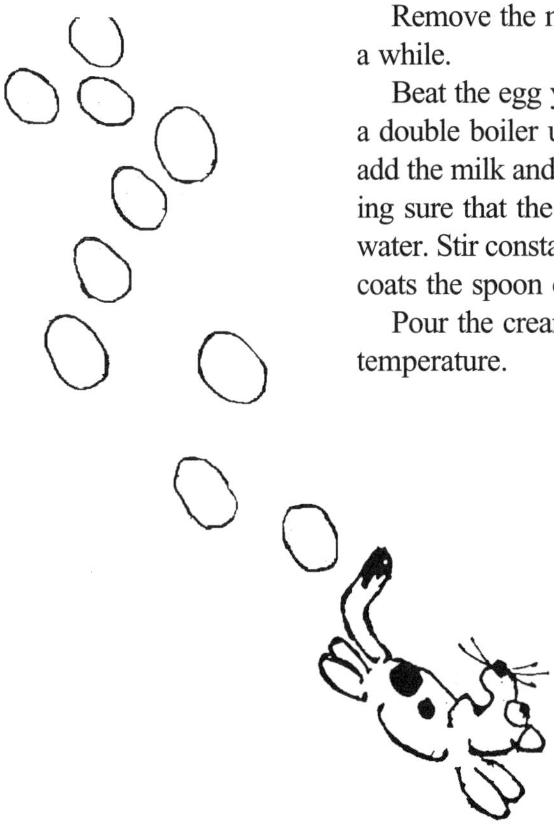

Place the milk and the lemon peel in a large saucepan and bring to a simmer. Meanwhile beat the egg white with salt until stiff, then, while beating, gradually add the confectioners sugar.

With a large spoon pick mounds of the white and drop them from the side of the spoon into the simmering milk, while trying to give each the shape of an egg. Turn the eggs so that they cook on all sides, and when they look firm—about 5 minutes—pick them with a slotted spoon, hold to drain and mound them on a serving plate.

Remove the milk from heat, strain it and let it cool for a while.

Beat the egg yolks with the sugar inside the top part of a double boiler until fluffy and lemon colored. Gradually add the milk and mix well. Cook over boiling water, making sure that the bottom of the top part doesn't touch the water. Stir constantly with a wooden spoon until the cream coats the spoon evenly.

Pour the cream over the snow eggs and serve at room temperature.

Serves 8.

UVETTA RICOPERTA DI CIOCCOLATA

CHOCOLATE-COVERED RAISINS (P)

I still have to find someone who doesn't like to munch on chocolate raisins. I still recall with pleasure the time when as children we feasted on them.

8 ounces semi-sweet chocolate
2 tablespoons pareve margarine
1 cup large seedless raisins

Dissolve the chocolate with margarine in a heavy-bottomed saucepan, stirring constantly. Turn off the heat, keep on stirring for a couple of minutes, then drop 1/2 cup raisins into the pan and stir with a fork to coat the raisins completely. Lift one by one and deposit on a piece of wax paper in a single layer. Reheat the chocolate slightly and keep on stirring, then repeat with the remaining 1/2 cup of raisins. Let cool to room temperature, then place in refrigerator for 10 to 15 minutes. Store in glass or plastic jar at room temperature. Use as snack or as garnish (they are ideal over a ricotta cake).

Yields 2 cups.

VIVA
VOV

VIN BRULÉ
HOT WINE (P)

When we were small children the only time we were allowed to drink wine was when we had a cold and our father prepared for us *vin brulé*, literally, burnt wine. The alcohol was lost in the boiling and the hot beverage was supposed to perform miracles in getting rid of our colds. We liked it so much that we almost welcomed a cold to have our father prepare for us this treat.

I am not sure why in Italy it is commonly designated with the French words *vin brulé* (the French actually call it *vin chaude*, hot wine), but I guess that many French words were brought to Italy by the world travelers at the turn of the century, (*comó, sofá, boudoir*, etc.) and many words stuck and it became chic to use them.

3 cups red wine
1 cooking apple, quartered
4 whole cloves
1/4 cup sugar
1 2-inch slice of lemon rind
1 stick, or 1 teaspoon ground, cinnamon

Place the wine in a saucepan with the apple studded with cloves, the sugar, lemon rind and cinnamon. Bring to a rapid boil and let cook, uncovered, for about 5 minutes. Filter it into glasses and serve hot.

Serves 6.

VOV I
SIMILAR TO EGG NOG (D)

This is the authentic, ancient recipe for this rich liquor as I have seen it being prepared when I was growing up in Italy. Since this was yet another of the many remedies used to bolster strength during convalescence, whole eggs were used because the calcium in the shell should not go to waste. In order to make sure that the eggs were absolutely fresh we got them from a neighbor who raised chickens in her vegetable garden. We picked them ourselves from the nest while still hot. Below I will also give the simpler version.

2 whole fresh eggs
1 cup acquavite
2 cups milk
1 teaspoon vanilla extract
1 1/2 cups sugar

Place 2 whole eggs in a large glass jar with acquavite and leave at room temperature for 2 weeks or until the shells dissolve. Shake vigorously.

Warm the milk with sugar and vanilla extract. Add to the liquor and shake well. Store at room temperature.

Yields about 3 1/2 cups.

VOV II
ITALIAN EGGNOG (D)

If you are as adventurous with foods as I am, you would want to try the above recipe. On the other hand, if you prefer to keep it simple, the following is a perfectly adequate way of making Vov.

Warm the milk with vanilla extract, then remove from heat and let cool to room temperature.

Beat the egg yolks with sugar until frothy and lemon colored. Pour in the acquavite mixing well until homogeneous. Gradually add the brandy, mixing. Lastly, add the aromized milk to the mixture. Store in a dark bottle at room temperature. Shake well before serving.

Yields 1 quart.

2 cups milk
1 teaspoon vanilla extract
4 egg yolks
1 1/2 cups sugar
1 cup acquavite
1/2 cup brandy

Z

ZABAIONE
(P OR D)

5 egg yolks
3/4 cup sugar
3/4 cup Marsala wine
2 tablespoons rum

Beat the egg yolks with sugar until pale-lemon colored. Gradually add the Marsala and rum, and keep beating until smooth.

Pour into a heavy-bottomed pot and place over a moderately high heat. Cook, stirring constantly, until *zabaione* coats the spoon evenly. Be careful not to allow the cream to reach the boiling point.

Pour into flute glasses and serve immediately.

Serves 6.

ZABAIONE FREDDO
COLD ZABAIONE (D)

3 eggs, slightly beaten
1 1/4 cups sugar
2 cups heavy cream, warm
1/2 cup dry Marsala wine
1/4 cup best quality rum
1 teaspoon vanilla extract
1 pint strawberries

Place the eggs and sugar in a heavy-bottomed saucepan and mix well to combine. Gradually add the warm cream and place over moderately high heat, stirring constantly. When the mixture begins to steam (but not boil!) remove from heat and let cool a little, stirring occasionally.

Add the wine, rum and vanilla extract, and mix. Strain through a fine strainer. Place a few slices of strawberries at the bottom of each flute glass, then fill with *Zabione* and top with one whole strawberry. Refrigerate.

Serves 8.

ZUCCHERO VANIGLIATO
VANILLA-FLAVORED CONFECTIONERS SUGAR (P)

Whenever a recipe calls for vanilla-flavored sugar, it is always intended to be confectioners sugar rather than granulated sugar. Since I do not believe you can find it already prepared on the American market, here is how you can easily make your own. But be careful that you don't lose it as once happened to me!

In one of my cooking classes, I demonstrated how easy it was to prepare vanilla-flavored sugar, then I put the jar in the pantry for use in the next class. When the time came, though, the jar was nowhere to be found. I inquired around, but nobody had even seen it. The mystery was revealed when the director of the school came to tell me to be more careful when I closed the jars: she had found the sugar jar full of bugs and had to throw the whole thing away. The little pieces of precious vanilla beans had appeared to her myopic eyes as dead bugs!

2 cups confectioners sugar
2 whole vanilla beans, cut into 1-inch sections.

Place sugar and beans into an air tight glass jar and set aside at room temperature for at least 2 weeks before using.

Sift just the quantity of sugar you need, then replenish the jar with equal amount of new sugar. Return any pieces of beans that you might find in the sifter into the jar, cover tightly and put aside until next time.

Replace the beans with new ones every 3 or 4 months.

Yields 2 cups.

ZUCCOTTO ALLA RICOTTA
RICOTTA ZUCCOTTO(D)

Our dear friend Anita Adduci of Florence sent me this recipe for an ice-cream cake that is as unusual as it is delicious. Soon after receiving the recipe we were invited to a dinner party and I made it to bring as a present. I was a bit trepidant, since never had I made or even tasted this *zuccotto*. Needless to say, it was a smashing success.

2 egg yolks
1 cup sugar
2 teaspoons flour
1/2 cup milk, warm
Grated rind of 1 lemon
2 1/2 cups whole-milk ricotta
20 amaretti (page 28) or 10 graham crackers, finely crumbed
2 teaspoons almond extract (only if you use graham crackers)
1/2 cup Orange Elixir or Cointreau
1/4 cup chopped candied fruit peels
1/4 cup chocolate chips
1 chocolate sponge cake (recipe follows)

Use a small whisk to beat the egg yolks with 1/4 cup sugar in a small saucepan. Add the flour and the lemon zest and keep on beating. Gradually add the warm milk and whisk until homogeneous. Place on a moderately high heat and bring to a boil, stirring constantly. Cook for two minutes, then remove the cream from heat.

Whip the ricotta until smooth and creamy. Add the remaining sugar and keep on beating for a minute or two. Add cream and powdered amaretti or Graham crackers (with almond extract), 2 tablespoons of elixir, the candied peels, and chocolate chips. Mix to combine.

Cut the sponge cake horizontally into 2 disks. Reserve the bottom and cut the other into slices. Line a 2 1/2-quart mold in the shape of a cupola with aluminum foil, then line it with the cake slices. Sprinkle the slices with elixir, then pour all the ricotta mixture into it. Sprinkle the reserved cake disk with the remaining liquor and place it over the mold. Cover with foil and place in freezer. When ready to use leave at room temperature for about 1 hour. Unmold upside down on a cake plate and peel the aluminum foil off.

Serves 8.

PAN DI SPAGNA AL CIOCCOLATO

CHOCOLATE SPONGE CAKE (P)

6 eggs, separated
pinch salt
3/4 cup sugar
3/4 cup flour
1 cup unsweetened cocoa
1 teaspoon baking powder
1 teaspoon vanilla extract
Pareve margarine to grease the pan

Beat the egg whites with salt until firm peaks form. In a separate bowl beat the egg yolks with sugar. Sift together flour, cocoa and baking powder and gradually add to the bowl. Add the vanilla extract and 1/3 of the beaten whites to soften the batter. Fold in the remaining whites and pour into a greased 9-inch springform cake pan. Bake in preheated 350 °F for 30 minutes, or until a skewer inserted at center comes out dry. Use as directed for the *zuccotto* in the preceding recipe.

Serves 6.

ZUCCOTTO FIORENTINO
FLORENTINE ICE CREAM CAKE (D)

There are probably as many versions of this cake as there are *pasticcerie* in Florence. And many more, I am sure, are from the homes of people who make their own desserts. I am familiar with a number of them, out of which I have chosen the following two. You will find that this one is the easiest to make, especially if you use store-bought ice cream. However, you should try *Zuccotto alla Ricotta* as well, which is very different and exquisite.

If you have the equipment and you are versed in making ice cream, by all means make your own. Otherwise, store-bought ice cream is perfectly adequate for this cake, and you will not have to work too hard to have a scrumptious dessert.

1 recipe Gelato alla Crema *or*
1 quart vanilla ice cream slightly softened
1/4 cup diced candied citron peel
1/4 cup chocolate chips
1/2 cup rum
Pan di Spagna *or store-bought sponge cake, sliced*

Take the ice cream from the freezer and leave it at room temperature for about one hour before starting preparations. Mix it with citron peel, chocolate chips, and 1 tablespoon rum.

Sprinkle the inside of a mold in the shape of a cupola with rum, then line it with slices of sponge cake. Drizzle rum on the slices. Pour the softened ice cream mixture inside the lined bowl and close it with more slices of sponge cake, drizzled with the remaining rum. Cover the mold with aluminum foil and place in the freezer.

About 1 hour before serving, remove *zuccotto* from the freezer, then unmold upside down over a serving plate.

Serves 6.

ZUCCOTTO FIORENTINO CLASSICO

CLASSIC FLORENTINE ZUCOTTO (D)

1 9-inch round sponge cake
1/2 cup Orange Elixir or Cointreau
1 cup hazelnuts
1 cup milk
1 teaspoon vanilla extract
2 egg yolks
3 tablespoons sugar
8 ounces semisweet chocolate chips
1 tablespoon sweet butter
1 pint heavy cream
3 tablespoons vanilla-flavored sugar (page 234)

Cut the cake horizontally obtaining 2 disks. Reserve the bottom one and cut the other into slices.

Toast the hazelnuts under the broiler until the peels are quite black. Let them cool for a while, then peel by rubbing them between the palms of your hands. Chop very fine, and place this powder in a saucepan with the milk and vanilla extract. Bring to a gentle boil and cook, stirring constantly, for 10 minutes. Remove from heat, and filter through a fine strainer. You should have about 1/2 cup liquid.

Beat the egg yolks with sugar in a saucepan. Slowly add the warm hazelnut milk beating with a small whisk. Return to heat and keep on stirring; as soon as the cream begins to "smoke" remove from heat and mix in 1 tablespoon of elixir.

Place half the chocolate chips in a heavy-bottomed saucepan with butter and slowly heat stirring until the chocolate is melted. Add to the hazelnut cream and mix to combine.

Whip the heavy cream until soft peaks form. Spoon half of it in the hazelnut/chocolate cream, whisking until homogeneous.

Add confectioners sugar and the remaining 4 ounces chocolate chips to the remaining half of whipped cream and gently mix with a spatula.

Line a 2 1/2-quart mold in the shape of a cupola with the sponge cake pieces, sprinkled with Elixir. Tilting and rotating the mold, spoon the chocolate mousse over the sponge cake lining. Fill the hole at center with the whipped cream/chocolate chips mixture, top with the reserved cake disk, sprinkled with the remaining elixir. Cover with aluminum foil and freeze.

About 1 hour before serving, take the *zuccotto* from the freezer, leaving it at room temperature. Peel off the aluminum foil, unmold upside down and serve.

Serves 8.

ZUPPA INGLESE
ENGLISH SOUP (D)

When I was a little child, Mother would take me with her to visit the homebound and the sick on Shabbat afternoons. During one of these visits, bored and restless, I climbed a few steps and leaned on a little window that opened into a dark pantry. The window was not fastened and I fell three or four feet on my back. I did not hurt myself, but I was frightened and began to cry. In order to calm me down, the young lady in the house, gave me a serving of her divine *Zuppa Inglese.* To this day this remains one of my favorite desserts.

1 cup Alkermes or any bright-red liqueur
30 Savoiardi *or lady fingers*
Crema Pasticcera
3/4 cup strong coffee
2 tablespoons brandy
1 pint heavy cream
1/4 cup confectioners sugar
1 teaspoon vanilla extract

Soak 14 of the lady fingers in red liquor and line the bottom and sides of a straight-sided glass serving bowl. Pour half the cream into the lined bowl.

Combine the coffee and brandy; quickly dip 8 lady fingers in this mixture and cover the cream with them. Pour the remaining cream over the lady fingers, then top it with the last 8 lady fingers soaked in the coffee mixture.

Whip the heavy cream until soft peaks form; add confectioners sugar and vanilla extract and mix gently. Top the bowl with mounds of whipped cream. Refrigerate before serving.

Serves 12.

INDEXES

GENERAL INDEX

A

B

C

Q

R

S

INDEX OF DAIRY DESSERTS

INDEX OF PAREVE DESSERTS

I

J

L

M

N

O

P

U

V

W

Y

Z

Other books by Edda Servi Machlin

CLASSIC CUISINE OF THE ITALIAN JEWS I
CLASSIC CUISINE OF THE ITALIAN JEWS II
CHILD OF THE GHETTO